ALWAYS NEAR
LISTENING FOR LESSONS FROM GOD

Bill Bagents

CYPRESS
PUBLICATIONS

ALWAYS NEAR
Listening for Lessons from God
Published by Cypress Publications
an Imprint of Heritage Christian University Press

Copyright © 2019 by William Ronald Bagents

Manufactured in the United States of America

Cataloging-in-Publication Data
Bagents, Bill (William Ronald), 1956–
Always Near: Listening for Lessons from God / by Bill Bagents
p. cm.
Includes index.
ISBN 978-1-7320483-1-7 (pbk.)
1. Devotional literature. 2. Christian life—Churches of Christ authors.
I. Author. II. Title.
BV4801 .B27 2019 242.2—dc20 2019-933599

Cover design by Brittany McGuire

For information:
Cypress Publications
3625 Helton Drive
PO Box HCU
Florence, AL 35630
www.hcu.edu

Book layout by BookDesignTemplates.com © 2017

Other than becoming a Christian, marrying Laura Lynn Stegall Bagents remains—hands down—the best decision I've ever made. She knows me better than anyone and loves me anyway.

The Lord is righteous in all His ways,
Gracious in all His works.
The Lord is near to all who call upon Him,
To all who call upon Him in truth.

PSALM 145:17–18

CONTENTS

FOREWORD

Asaph had it right, when he wrote by inspiration, "But as for me, the nearness of God is my good; I have made the Lord God my refuge, that I may tell of all Your works" (Psa 73:28). Asaph had struggled with the apparent unfairness of life, especially the prosperity of the wicked. His faith had suffered. His feet had almost slipped. His heart had become bitter. It was only when he drew close to God that he found help and hope. There was his refuge, as well as the message he wanted to share with the world. Asaph discovered that, no matter what, God was always near.

The book you hold in your hand, *Always Near: Listening for Lessons from God,* illustrates and elaborates on that powerful theme. Like Psalm 73, it points to the Lord as the only perfect source of hope, joy, and purpose. It speaks to anyone who seeks a closer walk with God. Lloyd O. Sanderson called it, "a constant sense of Thy abiding presence, where'er I am, to feel that Thou art near." I treasure this book because of its subject.

I also treasure this book immensely because of the qualities, heart, and character of its author. Anyone who knows Bill Bagents as I do would surely concur.

Dr. Bagents's educational credentials are certainly impressive. He has multiple advanced degrees, including an M.A. in New Testament from Amridge University, an M.Ed. in Counselor Education from Auburn University, an M.Div. from Amridge University, and a D.Min. in Biblical Studies from Amridge University.

His academic, ministry, and missions accomplishments are also outstanding. He serves as Vice President for Academic Affairs at Heritage Christian University. There he teaches graduate courses in ministry and undergraduate courses in Old Testament, New Testament, ministry, counseling, and church leadership. He serves as an elder and associate minister with the Mars Hill Church of Christ in Florence, Alabama. He has taught in evangelistic and training efforts in the Philippines, Russia, Bangladesh, Nigeria, South Africa, Namibia, Albania, and Jamaica. Bill is a prolific and effective writer. You can see that just by thumbing through a few pages of this current volume. Prior to this project, however, he has written for various Christian periodicals and authored or co-authored several books.

Beyond all these attainments, the quality of Bill's life is exemplary. I first remember meeting him almost twenty years ago when we helped plan a "Light the Fire" area-wide evangelistic campaign in Florence with our friend, Dr. Steven Guy. Then Bill helped open the door for me to teach and serve as Dean of Students with him at the University. When the Mars Hill church invited me to preach regularly, I had the privilege of sharing that pulpit with Bill for a number of years. I benefited and grew from every sermon I heard him deliver.

I have spent countless hours in Bill's office, sharing experiences, blessings, and challenges. He has been and still is my confidential counselor. His faith, patience, wisdom, and humor have reminded me often, as the title of this book notes, that God is always near.

In 2006, Bill and I served as mission partners in Cape Town, South Africa, with our friends there, Phillip and Roslyn Hendricks. We had worked hard, and we were exhausted. In the Cape Town airport, as we were preparing to fly to Johannesburg and then home, Bill and I noticed a very talkative, American woman questioning a store clerk regarding some money that she thought might be counterfeit. She was very persistent, to say the least.

We had to wait a long time in the Johannesburg airport. There was a four-hour delay because an engine had to replaced. We saw the same talkative American there, and it looked like she might be on our flight. When Bill and I finally boarded the plane for the twenty-plus-hour trip back to the United States, we were not seated together. Guess who had the seat beside Bill? Right! It was that same woman! Guess who would spend that long flight patiently listening to, supporting, and to some extent counseling that woman as her new best friend? The flight had not even begun before she began telling Bill her troubles and receiving his wise advice! That's my friend, Bill. He is always ready for an extended counseling session with a new client!

Bill and his dear wife Laura have two sons, John and Allen. They drew near to God again and again, but never more so than when Allen became desperately ill. As the result of an unknown infection, Allen required and received a double lung transplant. Bill and Laura leaned on the Lord, continually traveling back and forth to be with Allen at Johns Hopkins Hospital in Maryland. Just over a year after the surgery, Allen died at the age of 24.

Through that trial, with its pain, tears, and loss, Bill and Laura still found God to be always near. Their faith in such a difficult time has inspired me and countless others to rely on Him. As a Christian, a minister, an educator, a counselor, a husband, and a father, Bill has found God to be always near. That is in part because Bill has kept himself near to God.

As you read the pages that follow, you will feel that you are sitting at the feet of this very remarkable man. You will sense his uncanny ability to see God's imprint in the most common of circumstances. You will chuckle repeatedly as his dry wit and humor hit home. You will admire his down-to-earth, clear discussion of matters that may otherwise seem quite complex. You will be drawn to his humble, self-deprecating comments about his own struggles.

His transparency will help you see yourself, and more than that, the God on whom he relies. His logic will sharpen your own thinking. His love for God and for you will make him your friend for life, as he is mine.

Cory Collins
Keller, Texas

PREFACE

As talented friends were helping bring this book to life, they asked me for a title. *Always Near: Listening for Lessons from God* both comes from and speaks to my heart. God is always near. My favorite verse affirming that truth is Psalm 146:18, "The Lord is near to all who call upon Him, to all who call upon Him in truth." We find God near when we call, but also find Him near when we think, when we open our eyes, and when we open our hearts.

Always Near: Listening for Lessons from God flows from a strong conviction that God is always teaching us. He is the Master Teacher, He loves to teach, and He knows we need His continual help. While we'd never detract from the powerful ways God speaks through the Bible, we know He also speaks through what some have called "the poetics of everyday life."

Through His providence and the vibrant, powerful, and interactive nature of His word, God provides an endless number of lessons within the warp and woof of everyday life. (I hope that sentence made you think of both Hebrews 4:12 and the parables of Jesus.) We see a stunning sunset or a flower in full bloom, and we think of Psalm 19. We see someone showing respect to the elderly, and we find ourselves in Luke 2 with aged Anna and Simeon. We hear either sweet, soft words or the clank of harshness, and we're in Proverbs 15:1. If we're listening, life keeps taking us back to God's truth and wisdom.

God is always near, always teaching. We're blessed to hear what God has to say. Learning to listen for lessons from God is a sweet and humbling adventure. It brings many moments of "What took me so long?" and "Why didn't I see that sooner?" It also brings moments of awe. I claim no special revelation. It should probably go without saying that I continue to miss more lessons than I hear. Still, I love James 1:17, "Every good and perfect gift is from above and comes down from the Father of lights." Everything around us should be processed through the wisdom of Scripture. Without apology, we welcome every lesson that helps us as a gift from God, as yet another wondrous expression of His grace. God is always near and always teaching. Take the time and make the effort to listen for His lessons. It's a blessed choice that will open countless doors.

I have no idea where I first read, "Nothing good is ever written; everything good is rewritten." Even if that isn't universally true, it's true of me. Laura Bagents, Whitney Burgess, Aläna Marks, and Debbie May have corrected a boatload of my mistakes and assisted with insights and much needed suggestions. Several of these articles have been notably improved by Cory Collins. All the remaining mistakes belong to me, but there's no way to tell you how much help I've had.

The co-editors of Heritage Christian University Press and Cypress Publications, Jamie Cox and Brad McKinnon, did tons of work on this project. From creative aspects to motivation and insistence to typesetting, the book doesn't exist without them.

I remain grateful to Heritage Christian University and the Mars Hill Church of Christ for putting up with me. I especially appreciate friends who have encouraged me to keep writing. I think they know that I'd shrink if I didn't.

Bill Bagents
Florence, Alabama

ALWAYS NEAR

A Strange Art

But let your "Yes" be "Yes," and your "No," "No." For whatever is more than these is from the evil one.

Matthew 5:37

"He tried weekly" might be a testimony to perseverance. In other words, he didn't get the job yet, but he tried weekly to secure a positive result. "He tried weakly" is likely an indictment of poor effort. In other words, he didn't get the job and never will because in the interview, he tried weakly.

"I can't tell you how much I think of him" is similar. It might be a great compliment meaning, "Words fail me as I seek to speak sufficiently highly of him." But it could be a major slam along the lines of, "I can't tell you how much I think of him, because I don't think of him at all" or "I can't tell you how much I think of him, because I don't think much of him."

I remember hearing of the guy who was "a real go-getter." He took his wife to work every morning, and at 5:00 p.m., he went back to get her. Some people bless us greatly by letting their yes be yes and their no be no. Others can't seem to muster a decisive word. They leave us both fatigued and uncertain.

We know there's a communication continuum. Some of us can be too blunt. Others of us can be "careful" to the point of being wishy-washy and utterly unclear. There's much happy, blessed, and encouraging space between those unhealthy extremes.

If a car leaves the road and is heading directly toward your group on the sidewalk, there's no time for nuance and contextualization. "Run" is the needed word. We need the same kind of clarity when we see people moving toward spiritual destruction (Jam 5:19–20).

Other situations are not right v. wrong or faithfulness v. sin scenarios. We might find friends struggling to make a choice between good options. In those cases, we should be much more cautious with our words. We don't pretend to know more than we know. There may be no way to know whether taking the job with Company A is better than taking the job with Company B. The real issue may not be the choice of companies; it's the bigger choice of living for Christ no matter which job we take.

I love the Robert Frost poem, "The Road Not Taken." It speaks to our ears as it supports the virtue of courage in seeing the options before us and stepping up to make the nobler choice. As Christians, our minds go to Matthew 7:13–14 and Philippians 3:7–11 as we apply Frost's principle spiritually. In that sense, the road "less traveled by" is solidly and essentially superior.

I've noticed several recent blogs that reference Frost's poem. It surprises me that none of them have made a counter-argument. Sometimes the road most traveled is the tried-and-true. Sometimes the road less traveled is less traveled for good reason. You've seen the Westerns where the wagon train leaves the trail, takes the shortcut, and disaster follows. In those cases, the principle to be followed is Jeremiah 6:16 and Proverbs 3:5–8. Don't invent a new road when God has already presented a highway of holiness (Isa 35:8). God is master of the strange art of communication. I so wish we could master the art of hearing Him.

Thrift Store Philosophy

I will praise You, for I am fearfully and wonderfully made.

Psalm 139:14

Thrift stores aren't the worst places to gain philosophical insights. A recent trip to a local shop named Blue Door yielded a slightly worn coaster bearing these words: "Always remember that you are unique, just like everyone else." That's hard to beat for 75 cents.

It's so easy to see ourselves as special. In the sense of Psalm 139:14 and John 3:16, that's great. It leads us to praise God. We are moved to appreciate all that He has done for us and all that He has put within us. Every resource, ability, capacity, and opportunity flows from Him. On a really good day, we can even see ourselves in some lesser version of the Esther role: "Yet who knows whether you have come to the kingdom for such a time as this?" (Esth 4:14) Praise God for making each of us one of a kind!

It's so easy to forget that everyone else can also assert his or her uniqueness. You're just as special in your eyes as I am in mine. But if I'm not careful, I'll say that with reservation. Secretly, I "know" I'm really just a little more special than you. In such bad moments, Romans 12:3 offers needed correction. What a blessing not to think of ourselves more highly than we ought to think. What a blessing to realize that your strengths and talents don't diminish and shouldn't threaten me. There's joy and harmony in each of us giving our best to God (Col 3:23–24).

I'm not supposed to miss the humor of the coaster. Isn't it funny that humor so often intersects important insights? My coaster provides a sweet reminder of the power of biblical tensions. So many truths are best understood as they are placed side by side and explored. I am special, but no more special than you. I am loved by God, but not more loved than you. I may have some unique talents or gifts, but so do you (1 Cor 12:12ff). Our uniqueness flows from God. Rightly valued and employed, it blesses us all.

It will bless us to consider and value both our sameness and our uniqueness. It will bless us to more fully understand both the complexity and the simplicity of our walk with God.

We are indeed unique:

- Only identical twins have the same DNA, but even identical twins aren't fully identical.

- We're told that no two of us have the same finger prints or retinal patterns.

- I know it's non-standard English, but "We're all unique, but some of us are uniquer." Everyone either is or has "that" friend, cousin, uncle, or aunt.

While unique, we're also "just like everyone else" in so many vital ways:

- We're all loved by God more than we know (John 3:16; Rom 5:6–8).

- We're all sin-damaged and sin-doomed without God (Rom 3:23; 6:23; 8:1).

- This world isn't anyone's "forever home" (1 Thess 4:13–18; 2 Pet 3:10).

- God wants us home with Him (Matt 11:28–30; 1 Tim 2:1–6).

18

Lemons and Lemonade

But seek first the kingdom of God and His righteousness, and all these things shall be added to you.

Matthew 6:33

Sometimes I like football a bit too much. In an effort to reduce stress and keep priorities in order, one year I missed a chunk of the New Year's Day bowl games shopping with my wife, Laura. It worked out just fine. We found some sweet gifts that we hoped to take to some super people in Cape Town, South Africa later that year. I found a couple of books that were even better than I thought they'd be. One of the books deals with hope and the other with sarcasm. It's a perfect pairing for a person who loves and lives irony.

Thinking of New Year's bowl games, for most of them, I'm blessed not to have a dog in the hunt. Whatever happens, happens, and I don't much care. Sad to say that there was a time when I cared way too much about games, polls, predictions, and such. I used to think that a game couldn't be completed unless I watched. How dumb is that?

In large measure we get to choose what we invest in, what we give to, and what we hurt over. One cost of being a fan is that you hurt when your team loses. With little things like games, we dust ourselves off, get back up, and move along to more important matters. No one always wins. And there's always next year.

When it comes to using lemons to make lemonade, I hope that I've finally learned:

- *God is good all the time.* With every disappointment, He can teach us something important about life. If we can't find another lesson, we can always be reminded to anticipate the perfection of joy in heaven.

- *Sometimes the other guy wins.* Let him enjoy his moment. Don't see his joy as demeaning toward you or as disrespectful of your feelings. *If the other guy is disrespectful, be glad that it's him and not you.* Don't sink to his level. Two wrongs not only don't make a right, they often make the beginning of a war.

- *God is great at helping us keep things in perspective.* Consider Ecclesiastes 12. Choose to appreciate and enjoy the blessings of each day and of each stage in life. Respect God above all. Remember Matthew 6:33. The needs and the good of the kingdom trump all other interests.

- *If a hobby, habit, or recreational interest stops blessing you, either drop it or cut it back.* That's not quitting. Rather, it's a strategic reallocation of resources. Adjust intelligently.

- *Don't put all hurts in the same category.* Let the little stuff be little. Save your heart of hearts for the things that really matter.

- *Never think of the pain of others as little.* To live BIG, we must love BIG (1 Pet 4:8).

We Are Smarter than Me

The fear of the Lord is the beginning of knowledge, but fools despise wisdom and instruction.

Proverbs 1:7

We have been known to buy a book for Heritage Christian University's Overton Memorial Library from time to time. We love to remember the Overtons, we like books, and we enjoy opportunities to contribute to learning. One of our latest finds was *We Are Smarter than Me.*

Because book titles can't be protected by copyright, there could be several books with this title. We wouldn't mind that at all. Many seem to have forgotten the basic truth this title asserts. We regularly encounter or read about individuals who think they're both smarter and wiser than all those around them. They value their perspective and preferences to the exclusion of other possibilities. Such thinking does not fit Scripture:

- "The fear of the Lord is the beginning of knowledge, but fools despise wisdom and instruction" (Prov 1:7).

- "The fear of the Lord is the beginning of wisdom" (Prov 9:10).

- "Lord, I know the way of man is not in himself; it is not in man who walks to direct his own steps" (Jer 10:23).

- Remember Rehoboam in 1 Kings 12. He requested and received solid counsel but rejected it because it did not fit his agenda.

- "For I say, through the grace given to me, to everyone who is among you, not to think of himself more highly than he ought to think, but to think soberly, as God has dealt to each one a measure of faith" (Rom 12:3).

We are smarter than me, and God is infinitely wiser and more knowledgeable than all of us. And the implications of these statements are easy to state: Listen to God. Read and heed His revelation. Ask God for wisdom.

- Listen to others, particularly to godly people whose consistent lives show us their faith and understanding.

- Listen to others, as God can use any source anywhere and anytime to help us. Listen critically and evaluate everything using the Bible as the standard; but choose to listen.

The devil is the master of twisting every truth. How might he twist "we are smarter than me"?

- "We are smarter than me. Therefore, always go with the majority. There's safety in numbers. Never trust yourself more than the consensus that surrounds you." How'd that work out for Noah and his family? How'd that work out for the ancient Israelite nation as it followed the ten spies rather than the two?

- "We are smarter than me. Therefore, if I follow the majority and stick with the crowd, God will have no standing to judge me even if I'm wrong in my actions or understanding." God never lacks standing to hold His creation responsible for its actions.

- "We are smarter than me. Therefore, it's dangerous to study the Bible for yourself. You could be wrong in your process or your outcomes. Best to leave such matters to professionals." This assertion is the opposite of Acts 17:11 and 2 Timothy 3:13–17.

We need God's wisdom and help from God's people to avoid pride that would have us destroy ourselves. It's far too easy to tell ourselves what we want to hear and think we are right.

Being a Contrarian

But what things were gain to me, these I have counted loss for Christ. Yet indeed I also count all things loss for the excellence of the knowledge of Christ Jesus my Lord, for whom I have suffered the loss of all things, and count them as rubbish, that I may gain Christ.

Philippians 3:7–8

My tendency toward contrarian thinking often works to prevent boredom. For example, I got the following as part of a solicitation to purchase parenting materials: "Although you may not realize it, you have two choices when confronted with difficult children:

- You can continue to parent as if your child is the child you dreamed of parenting.

- You can develop the skills necessary to parent the child you actually have."

Clever wording, but it immediately challenges my contrarian nature. The ad presents two choices as if they were the only options. From a marketing perspective, it stacks the deck strongly toward the more productive of the two. I'd never recommend any of them, but other choices exist:

- One could quit parenting altogether and leave the child to his own devices. While Proverbs 29:15 clearly condemns this approach, some parents still take it.

- One could homogenize, moving toward the illusion of "I parent all my children exactly alike." Never works, not even with identical twins. No two children are ever exactly alike. Even if they were, their circumstances and life experiences wouldn't be.

- One could bounce from one parenting approach to another. I've heard such defended under the ideas of "keep the kids confused, so you can maintain the upper hand" and "you never know what might work until you try it." I hope the weaknesses of these "arguments" are obvious.

Perhaps you think of other options. Even if you don't, the false dichotomy of the email solicitation has been exposed. Still, the language of the advertisement offers food for thought.

There's the phrase "difficult children." Virtually all children are "difficult" in some ways at some times. I've heard stories of stunning exceptions, but such stories are stunning because they're so rare.

Unrealistic expectations don't bless us. They don't assist in helpful decision making. They bring unhealthy stress and frustration. Denial is powerful. Wishing things (or people) were different does not change reality. What is is, whether that's good, bad, desirable, undesirable, helpful, or frustrating.

Better skills can be learned. None of us, not even the parent of the most difficult child—or the child of the most difficult parents—is stuck without options. If we can change nothing else, we can change our perspective and our attitude with God's help. 2 Corinthians 12 and Philippians 3–4 offer three stunning examples from Paul's life. Genesis 50:20 offers a strong example from Joseph's. We'd never claim that this process is easy, but we're confident that it's blessed.

Observe by Watching

Walk in wisdom toward those who are outside, redeeming the time. Let your speech always be with grace, seasoned with salt.

Colossians 4:5–6

"You are the light of the world.... Let your light so shine before men that they may see your good works and glorify your Father in heaven" (Matt 5:14, 16). "Walk in wisdom toward those who are outside, redeeming the time. Let your speech always be with grace, seasoned with salt" (Col 4:5–6).

Yogi Berra was right about a lot of things. It's difficult to top his quote that's the title of this article. My father's accompanying quote is, "There ain't nothin' folks won't do." I wish I could say that wasn't true.

Recently, we were plundering—for our first and last time—in a "wanna be" antique store. Another customer entered and started talking to the proprietor in a stage whisper: "He bought her a ring. He made me promise not to tell anybody. He made me promise not to tell you, but I had to tell somebody. I don't know when he'll give it to her. She has a birthday in August."

For crying out loud. She was telling the untellable with details in a public place and confessing that she had no right to blab even as she was blabbing. I don't know who "he" is, but none of his business will ever be private or secure. That's somewhere past sad. When you can't trust your own family, it hurts your heart and your soul. Chances are that when "he" figures this out, no more secrets will be shared. And she won't know why she's always left out of the loop.

Our next stop was a used bookstore. Laura asked the clerk a few questions, and she made a friend for life. He shared about family history, his careers, his favorite foods, travel plans, the upcoming community yard sale, favorite authors, and more. None of it was out of place. Laura found it quite interesting on one level, and I agreed on another. We talk about what's important to us. Most people love to tell their stories.

We had seen that in action the night before at dinner. The cashier who took our order wanted us to see the large table of folks right behind us. Those were her people. And her daughter had just told her that she was pregnant. Her punch line was, "Best Mother's Day gift ever!" The lady didn't know us from Adam, but she needed for us to share her moment. We were happy to do so.

In the bookstore later that evening, we weren't sure if the guy near the register was in line or just browsing, so Laura asked. He didn't know either. I thought he spoke too sharply to his wife who was a few steps away, looking at cards as she waited. She stepped closer to him to preserve her place in line. My first thought was, "I don't think this is the first time he's spoken too sharply to her." My second thought was, "I need to take this as a lesson to watch my own mouth. Is God using this moment to teach me?" My kindness quotient isn't always where it should be either.

Our last stop that evening was the grocery store. As we entered the checkout line, the cashier said, "Bill Bagents. You teach at Heritage Christian." I recognized her as the girlfriend of an HCU student. I was glad I was on good behavior. People may see more of us and in us than we realize. They may recognize us long before we see them. And that won't trouble us at all if we're behaving as Christians ought. People indeed observe a lot by watching us.

Fried Peaches

But be doers of the word, and not hearers only, deceiving yourselves.

James 1:22

The "Fried Peaches" label caught my eye. I like peaches, and I like fried. What's not to like? At $1.50 and 20% off, it was worth a try. I'll admit disproportionate disappointment. The peaches weren't fried—just plain old canned peaches. Even the "heating directions" on the label didn't involve frying. Heat on medium in a saucepan while stirring, or "nuke" (my word) two minutes on high in the microwave.

So comes the question: Why did the label say "Fried Peaches"? You know the answer. Now, even I know the answer. The label tells you what you want to hear to get you to make the purchase. Misleading? Definitely. A lie? I think so. Effective? Only once with me. *Caveat emptor* remains true and important.

I'm not sure the peach company learned this directly from the devil, but the misleading, deceptive label clearly follows his MO. Forget the facts; just tell people what they want to hear. It's as old as Eve in the garden with the snake—different fruit, same approach.

Rampant deception and dishonesty serve to make us even more impressed with God's consistent clarity and truthfulness. This fact is so obvious in the ministry of Jesus.

- He identified and challenged individual hypocrisy (Matt 7:1–5).

- He stoutly warned the self-deceived (Matt 7:21–23).

- He praised great examples of faith, even when they involved inconvenient people (Matt 8:5–13).

- He stayed "on mission" even when critics lashed out (Matt 9:9–13).

- He rebuked those in need of rebuke (Matt 11:20–24).

- He publicly challenged errant teaching, even when He knew that some would be offended (Matt 15:1–14).

- He challenged faithlessness, even among His closest disciples (Matt 16:8–12).

- He strongly praised right words and right actions, even when they came from flawed followers (Matt 16:13–23).

- He identified and challenged institutional hypocrisy (Matt 23).

- He clearly stated the cost of discipleship (Luke 9:23–26), and its rewards (John 14:1–6).

- He even chose to share His heartbreak over those who refused His salvation (Matt 23:37–39).

No misleading. No falsity. No deceit. Love and honesty always.

Just Go With It

Therefore let us pursue the things which make for peace and the things by which one may edify another.

Romans 14:19

A ll the books were priced in even dollars. I had two calendars at 50-cents each. They don't charge sales tax, but the gentleman announced the total purchase as $16.20. I paid him $16.20. Though that math doesn't come close to working, sometimes it's just better to go with it. He was happy, I was happy, and neither of us needed to re-check. I'll never know whether I got a discount or made a contribution.

Perhaps my tolerance for ambiguity is finally growing toward a healthy level. Maybe I'm finally admitting that life doesn't always make sense. Maybe I'm learning that some questions aren't worth asking. Sometimes, it's okay just to let things be. It could be that the following passages are being honored and applied:

- "Love ... does not behave rudely, does not seek its own, is not provoked, keeps no accounts of evil" (1 Cor 13:4–5).

- "Therefore let us pursue the things which make for peace and the things by which one may edify another" (Rom 14:19).

- "If it is possible, as much as depends on you, live peaceably with all men" (Rom 12:15).

- "The discretion of a man makes him slow to anger, and his glory is to overlook a transgression" (Prov 19:11).

We know that "slow to anger" is almost always a virtue. We also know that sometimes it's even better to forego anger entirely. Every potential fight is not worth fighting.

There are far more serious situations, where we are blessed to "just go with it" and not raise a stink. Think of 1 Corinthians 6.

Paul's stunning questions to those in legal battles with brethren were, "Why do you not rather accept wrong? Why do you not rather let yourselves be cheated?" Paul was not belittling honesty and righteousness. Rather, he was promoting personal sacrifice for the sake of the kingdom. Paul knew that God would more than make up for any loss they suffered.

Think also of Hebrews 10:34. The writer praised those who "joyfully accepted the plundering of your goods knowing that you have a better and an enduring possession for yourselves in heaven." He praised their perspective, sacrifice, wisdom, and faith. By foregoing an earthly battle that they could not have won, they made major deposits in the treasury of heaven.

We don't compromise truth and principle. We don't stand by and let others be hurt if we have a godly way to intervene. But we don't fight every battle as if it were a matter of life and death. We don't try to win every situation and circumstance. Sometimes, a gracious loss is superior. Sometimes a gracious loss or a non-battle follows the supreme example of Christ (1 Pet 3:18–25). May God bless us with the wisdom to know what's right and the courage to do it!

Opinions

Judge not, that you be not judged. For with what judgment you judge, you will be judged; and with the measure you use, it will be measured back to you.

Matthew 7:1–2

A friend from South Africa recently sent me the British version (the spellings give that away) of a story I first heard long ago. Sorry I don't know the author to be able to give proper credit.

Judging others and forming an opinion is easy. The following narrative was told of a newly married young couple.

They moved into a new neighbourhood. The next morning while they were eating their breakfast, the young woman saw her neighbour hanging out her washing.

"That laundry is not very clean," she said. "She doesn't know how to wash correctly. Perhaps she needs better laundry powder."

Her husband looked on but remained silent.

Every time her neighbour would hang the washing to dry, the young woman would make the same comments.

About a month went past, and the woman was surprised one morning, when she saw the nice sparkling clean washing on the line and said to her husband, "Look, she has learnt to wash correctly. I wonder who taught her this?"

Her husband said, "I got up early this morning and cleaned our windows."

And so it is with life. What we see when watching others depends on the purity of the windows we look through. Let us not be prejudiced when looking at others. Choose to see also the good. Do not allow our opinions to cloud our judgment. After reading this narrative, the most appropriate Scripture that came to mind was Matthew 7:1–5. We also think of John 7:24 and the Parable of The Good Samaritan.

I'm glad my friend sent the story and his comments. Jumping to conclusions often breaks things—including the Golden Rule and the second greatest commandment. All of us have experienced the realization that the problem of the moment wasn't at all what we had assumed. Most of us have also realized at times that the "problem" of the moment was us.

Given general human limitations and the influence of this sin-damaged world, all of us look at others through dirty windows. That calls us to appreciate James 1:5 and 1:19–20 all the more. It also brings greater appreciation of Philippians 2:3–4. Only God sees with perfect clarity. And He chooses to love us anyway!

Seasons of Refreshing

Repent therefore, and be converted, that your sins may be blotted out, so that times of refreshing may come from the presence of the Lord.

Acts 3:19–20

I love Peter's sermon in the temple as recorded in Acts 3. It has much kinship with the Pentecost sermon of Acts 2. Peter pulls no punches. His hearers had denied and killed the Holy One of God, but God had great news for them. God raised the Prince of life and offers new life (conversion and refreshing) through Him. That gospel offer will stand as long as this world stands.

"Times of refreshing" that come "from the presence of the Lord" are always welcome. They begin when God moves us from dead in sin to alive in His Son (Rom 6:1-14; Eph 2:1-10). They begin with our conversion; but if we stay faithful in Christ, they never end.

A recent week had been three Mondays in a row. Aggravations and frustrations led to fatigue on every level. It was Wednesday night and approaching time for Bible class. And the season of refreshing began.

Sweet friends who might face far more trouble than I do showed up for Bible class with sweet spirits, good attitudes, and encouraging words. Some of them had spent the day waiting with brethren during surgery and caring for family members. They brought good news of medical successes and better news of Christians showing second-mile service to the glory of God. Their conduct and their comments served "to stir up love and good works" (Heb 10:24).

The Bible class wasn't just structured to welcome comments from the congregation; it was built to depend on insights and application from fellow students. Those insights and applications proved impressively refreshing. Every comment was on task and helpful. We could feel ourselves drawing energy from God's truth and our effort to hear it. It was a sweet time that left us feeling blessed to be with the saints.

Given the week of Mondays, it would not do to know the results of an honest impromptu poll. "How many of you are way tired tonight?" "How many of you had to summon extra energy to get here this evening?" A couple of extra-honest folks even commented, "I'm not sure if I'll be able to stay awake this evening." And I believe that we all left feeling better than when we came—refreshed by hearing God's word and being with God's people. More than that, we were refreshed by being together in the presence of the Lord.

Not every Bible class feels as successful as the one we mention above. Not every worship assembly connects emotionally as well as this particular Wednesday evening did. But it sure is sweet when seasons of refreshing come together in such an obvious way. It gives us occasion to thank God for loving us, saving us, adding us to His church, and allowing us to encourage one another as we worship Him. God is good, and He loves sending seasons of refreshing.

It Goes Without Saying

But concerning brotherly love you have no need that I should write to you, for you yourselves are taught by God to love one another.

1 Thessalonians 4:9

I promise I read it online from a TV station's homepage some time back. The title for one of the posts was, "High pollen count not good for people with allergies." I admit it made me think.

- If that's part of today's news, nothing at all must be happening.

- Is the high pollen count somehow good for people who don't have allergies?

- Do you really think people with allergies are unaware of their suffering or its cause?

Some things seem so obvious that they could easily go without saying.

- *Don't take our new wonderful medication if you are allergic to it or any of its ingredients.* Common sense agrees. And is there anything you should take if you are allergic to it?

- *Take our new wonderful medication, but don't exceed the recommended dosage.* I guess that's to protect the more-is-always-better people.

- *Take our new wonderful medication, but stop taking it if it impairs your breathing.* Breathing has always seemed important. Captain Obvious is in the house!

Now I find myself wanting to create my own list of things that go without saying.

- *Don't play with sin.* Sin and its consequences often don't stop "playing" when we're ready to stop (Rom 6:23). Remember the David and Bathsheba story.

- *Don't treat people badly* (Matt 22:38–39). God's laws of sowing and reaping apply—always (Gal 6:7–8). God loves people, but sin always costs.

- *Don't try to game God.* God isn't gameable. He already knows all the motives, all the moves, and all the outcomes (Psa 139:1–4). Those who think they're gaming God are always only gaming themselves.

- *Tell the truth.* We don't have to tell all that we know. We don't have to tell all that we think. We don't have to answer every question that's asked. But what we say must be true (Eph 4:25; John 8:44; Matt 5:37).

- *Do right.* When it's hard, do right. When it's costly, do right. When others disagree, do right. When it seems to pay more to do wrong, do right (Col 3:17, 23–24).

- *Don't give up on God.* Don't give up on faith, hope, and love. Don't give up on heaven. Don't give up on God's power to save. "Be faithful until death, and I will give you the crown of life" (Rev 2:10). "There is laid up for me the crown of righteousness, which the Lord, the righteous Judge, will give me on that Day, and not to me only, but also to all who have loved His appearing" (2 Tim 4:8).

Thinking Inside the Box

"For My thoughts are not your thoughts, nor are your ways My ways," says the Lord. "For as the heavens are higher than the earth, so are My ways higher than your ways, and My thoughts than your thoughts."

Isaiah 55:8–9

My great-nephew was almost four. He had a sister who was almost two. Nephew had a logical dilemma over the approaching birth of a second sister. He wanted to keep the sister he already had and to welcome the new sister, but "You can't put two babies in one crib—won't fit." He had put himself in a box as a three-year-old logician. Within his zero-sum world, there was no solution.

Jesus faced adults with zero-sum thinking. Remember the following examples:

- Jesus claimed to be the Messiah, but Scripture says the Messiah will come from Bethlehem (John 7:42). Since Jesus came from Nazareth, His claim must be false. It never occurred to the critics that one can be born in one city but reared in another.

- It took 46 years to build the temple that stood in Jesus' day. Jesus said, "Destroy this temple, and in three days I will raise it up" (John 2:19). Critics were incredulous (Mark 14:58). It never occurred to his critics that He was speaking of "the temple of His body" (John 2:21).

- Jewish folks in Jesus' day knew that the Messiah remains forever (John 12:34). Given that, Jesus' prediction of His death meant that He could not be the Messiah. That which is forever cannot die. It seems that they never considered the possibility of the resurrection.

We have encountered similar modern "logic":

- God cannot be tempted with sin (Jam 1:13). Jesus was "in all points tempted as we are, yet without sin" (Heb 4:15). Therefore, Jesus cannot be God. But we know John 1:1–2 says otherwise. We know the answer lies in the fact that Jesus was God in the flesh (Phil 2:5–8).

- Salvation is by grace through faith, not of works (Eph 2:8–9). Therefore, no human work, even baptism, can have any role in salvation. But we know that 1 Peter 3:21 says: "There is an antitype which now saves us— baptism." We know that Acts 2:38, 22:16, and Romans 6:1–4 link baptism and salvation. The answer? Scripture tells us that it is God who works in our baptism. In baptism we are "raised with Him through faith in the working of God, who raised Him from the dead" (Col 2:12).

- Similarly, some reason that works have nothing to do with either salvation or faithful living (Eph 2:9). Don't you wish they'd remember to read just one verse further? Obviously, we're not saved by works of merit. We're not saved by our works at all. But "we are His workmanship created in Christ Jesus for good works." We are to abound in the work of the Lord (1 Cor 15:58). Faith is dead without works (Jam 2:17).

- Some assert that since gospel means "good news," it cannot be obeyed. It can be believed and welcomed, but not obeyed. Yet 2 Thessalonians 1:8 and 1 Peter 4:17 beg to differ.

And the key question is—will I trust my limited logic above God's holy word?

Luggage Language

Therefore take heed how you hear.

Luke 8:18a

It caught my ear when a coworker recently used the phrase "luggage language." Given the oddities of my mind, I've been thinking about it ever since.

The TSA people at the airport love to ask, "May I open your bag?" Everybody knows it's not really a question. They're opening the bag no matter what you say. It's rhetorical, like "What shall a man give in exchange for his soul?" or "Shall not the judge of all the earth do right?"

When you fly, there are both size and weight limits on your luggage. You can fly overweight if you have enough credit card to cover the extra cost. Sometimes you can even pay for an extra bag, but you can't put more in a bag than the physical space allows. And the airline's idea of oversize isn't necessarily mine. It's okay to ask for grace, but it's never wise to argue.

When you fly, be nice. I weigh bags at home, but I don't always get it right. Several times, I've been a pound or two over and been "green lighted" anyway. I love it when that happens. Unexpected kindness tends to have a very positive effect on most of us—at least it should.

"Keep a bag packed" can be positive luggage language. It could mean, "I might be coming by to get you. We'll have a great trip." On the other hand, there's, "We wouldn't want to start the surgery without you being here" or "You never know when things will get so bad that you have to leave without warning."

"Pack your bag and go home" is just as broad a phrase. Think of the happy person who's being released from the hospital following life-saving surgery. On the other hand, think of the evils of someone sending a spouse away forever.

"Fragile" or "Handle with Care" are two of my least favorite luggage language terms. I think baggage handlers read these as challenges. Both labels say to them, "Let's see how hard we can slam this one!" or "If I don't hear a shattering sound, I'll be disappointed.   I have a friend who owns an extra-large suitcase. Back when, his wife warned him before a major mission trip, "Don't overload that big piece; you'll hurt your back." She didn't mean to be prophetic. He eventually recovered.

On a very early mission trip, a friend cautioned me, "Don't put all your stuff in a single bag. If that bag gets lost, you'll be in trouble." I have always heeded that good advice. Funny thing is that he didn't heed his own advice. He wore the same shirt for some ten days before they found his bag. It made for interesting photos. Knowing what to do isn't the same as doing what we know to be best.

I can remember when I first started flying overseas for mission trips. I had no clue what to do about luggage. Now I know— never lock anything. Even if the lock works well, it's no trouble to slice a piece of canvas. The uglier the better. If it's not scratched and dented when you leave for the airport, it soon will be. Function matters more than form. The question is not "How does it look?" The better question is, "Does it work?" or "Will it get the job done?"

Is This Place Good?

Therefore, as we have opportunity, let us do good to all, especially to those who are of the household of faith.

Galatians 6:10

On a rainy Saturday, we drove to a local steakhouse. The man entering behind us asked, "Is this place good?" He had no idea what a fine question he was asking.

During the meal, the man sitting directly behind me seemed developmentally disabled. Every employee who walked by spoke to him. Their attention and attitudes were exemplary. There was no hint of condescension. There was no sense of feeling bothered. Since he was in their restaurant, he was their customer, treated with full respect and extra concern.

The other cool thing was that all the employees were very young. (I know that compared to me, virtually everybody is young; but these seemed extra-young.) And their behavior was exemplary. They blessed our meal and blessed our hearts.

There may be some huge backstory that we don't know. It doesn't matter if there is. What we saw was sweet and special. What we saw made the restaurant a very good place on that day.

You'd be right to think, "But this is the way it should be—always!" But have you noticed how seldom things are just the way they should be? This world is often unkind, even cruel. We've reached a point where kindness seems so rare and more obviously special.

We don't want that to be true of us. We want to be known for love, grace, mercy, kindness, and respect. God would have it no other way.

- "But do not forget to do good and to share, for with such sacrifices God is well pleased" (Heb 13:16).

- "Let your speech always be with grace, seasoned with salt" (Col 4:6). "But above all things put on love, which is the bond of perfection" (Col 3:14).

- "Therefore be imitators of God as dear children. And walk in love, as Christ also has loved us and given Himself for us" (Eph 5:1–2).

- "Be kindly affectionate to one another with brotherly love, in honor giving preference to one another, not lagging in diligence, fervent in spirit, serving the Lord" (Rom 12:10–11).

- "You shall love your neighbor as yourself" (Matt 22:39).

"Is this place good?" Every place is better when God is there. God is ever present in His faithful people.

Oddities

A merry heart does good, like medicine, but a broken spirit dries the bones.

Proverbs 17:22

One of my pastimes has been shopping for bargains at a local store where the prices decline every ten days—at least they used to decline. The last time I visited, I learned that they have changed their business model. The signs and dated labels are gone. Where's the fun in that?

We went to Walmart recently to pick up some cheap colas through their price match with local competitors. At checkout, we learned that they stopped their price match program last September. Who knew? Apparently, everybody in Florence except me.

As we ate out one day, the hostess walked us past "umpteen" (that's one of my favorite numbers) empty tables all the way to the back corner so that we could sit by the couple with the five rowdy children. The longer we sat, the rowdier they got. While it wasn't a pleasant meal, we found considerable joy in knowing they weren't our relatives and none of them were going home with us. There's generally both a silver lining and a reason to give thanks if you look hard enough.

As we ate out some days later, a young couple with two little kids were seated next to us. My first thought was a dismal, "Here we go again." To my surprise the kids behaved perfectly. On the way out, we interrupted their meal to congratulate the parents on the civility of their children. It's a pleasure to see parents making good effort and winning.

A friend set up an appointment for people from HCU to look at some furniture in a lawyer's office in downtown Tuscumbia. We got a bookcase and a table for the Overton Memorial Library. The coolest purchase of the day was personal—two wooden billy clubs. They were on the floor by the table. In that it never hurts to ask, I inquired. The attorney's father had been a policeman; the clubs had been his. The seller suggested an acceptable price, and I now have two new-to-me high character antiques plus a 48-inch ruler. All that, and I have no plans to threaten, smite, or anyone.

What are the take-aways from this latest round of oddities?

- *Change is constant.* Sometimes it's good, sometimes bad, but it's relentless either way. That which does not change is rare and precious (Jam 1:17; Psa 119:89; Mal 3:6).

- *Pleasant surprises are always welcome.* It's good to find them, but it's even better to cause them.

- *We really can find a reason for thankfulness in every situation*, but some situations require much more faith, effort, perspective, and creativity than others (1 Thess 5:18; Phil 4:10–13).

- *We can't predict the value that people place on pieces of their history.* You know the saying, "One man's trash...." I love the accompanying saying: "Never price anything that you don't want to sell." I'm trying not to live down to "A fool and his money are soon parted."

New Words

These are the things you shall do: speak each man the truth to his neighbor; give judgment in your gates for truth, justice, and peace.

Zechariah 8:16

Every field or discipline tends to have its own specialized vocabulary. That seems to be one way of differentiating between insiders and outsiders. Sometimes it gets to be quite strange.

I remember the first time I was told that a hospital patient had expired. Warranties expire. Subscriptions expire. The "use by" date on medications expire. I don't tend to think of people expiring. I remember when an apple and a blackberry were just things that you ate. Sometimes words get reassigned or expanded in unforeseen ways.

In years gone by, Librarian Jamie Cox would weed titles from the Overton Memorial Library. She removed obsolete or unneeded books. OML even had an official weeding policy. I recently learned that librarians no longer weed. Now, they deselect. The current debate seems to be whether they deselect or de-select. We chose to omit the hyphen in the spirit of simplicity.

Governments seem to love new words and new phrases. Politicians don't support tax increases, but they love to enhance revenue. They support transparency on a need-to-know basis. They'll describe a plane crash as "a sudden unscheduled landing." Recession gets re-labeled as "prolonged economic downturn." A military retreat becomes a "strategic redeployment of personnel."

Games with words can be fun, but not when the goal of the game is to mislead or manipulate. We see such games condemned by Christ in Matthew 23:16–22. We love the clear words of Jesus from Matthew 7:37, "But let your 'Yes' be 'Yes,' and your 'No,' 'No.' For whatever is more than these is from the evil one."

2 Timothy 2:14 is so helpful: "Remind them of these things, charging them before the Lord not to strive about words to no profit, to the ruin of the hearers." Many Bibles link the verse to Titus 3:9: "But avoid foolish disputes, genealogies, contentions, and strivings about the law; for they are unprofitable and useless."

Old or new, we will be judged by our words. "A good man out of the good treasure of his heart brings forth good things, and an evil man out of the evil treasure brings forth evil things. But I say to you that for every idle word that men speak, they will give account in the day of judgment. For by your words you will be justified, and by your words you will be condemned" (Matt 12:35–37). Consider the following implications:

- Our words are a window to our hearts.

- God knows both our words and our hearts.

- We are responsible for both our words and the hearts from which they flow.

- We will give account to God in the judgment.

In light of that, Proverbs 10:19 and 17:27 bless us: "In the multitude of words, sin is not lacking, but he who restrains his lips is wise." "He who has knowledge spares his words."

Funny Math

For what profit is it to a man if he gains the whole world, and is himself destroyed or lost?

Luke 9:25

I sometimes do okay with simple math where the numbers are numbers and they all sit on the same line. I'm no good at all when you step to the quadratic equation or the $f(x) = y$. There are many forms of math that don't work for me.

Have you seen the online "length of life" calculators? You get to add a year for exercise but smoking or a family history of heart disease makes you subtract. My favorite related quote came from a friend who did the calculations and reported, "According to this, I've been dead for four years and didn't know it."

I recently read a news item from my home county. Two teens were charged with one count of murder and three counts of attempted murder after shooting into a vehicle occupied by a man and a woman. That math doesn't work. Two days later the story was amended to say the truck that they fired into was occupied by a total of four people. That emendation temporarily restored some sense of balance to my limited mathematical life.

I like the story of the self-congratulatory preacher who was bragging to his wife about what a fine sermon he had delivered. Finally, he asked her, "How many people would say that was the best sermon ever?" Her response: "At least one less than you think." Math can be painful.

I remember "back when" hearing two brethren speaking very critically of a mission trip. "All that money spent, and there were only three baptisms." My understanding has always been that we can't put a price on a soul. Luke 9:25 supports that. Would I have preferred 30 or 300 baptisms? Sure, but I have no reason and no desire to discount the importance of those three.

The Lord has blessed me to preach to a few crowds of some size, but I've also preached to a "crowd" of three. In some senses it's easier to speak to the bigger group, but I'd never claim that it's more important. Think of Acts 8 and the Spirit sending Philip to find the Ethiopian man. One seeker got God's attention and led God to act. The same truth is taught in Luke 15:4 as the shepherd leaves ninety-nine safe sheep to "go after the one which is lost until he finds it."

There are so many forms of "funny" math. One of the devil's favorites goes like this: "I'll have multiple opportunities to repent. Skipping one won't matter. No need to feel any pressure or to be in any hurry." Ask Uzzah about that. Ask Ananias and Sapphira. In God's grace, many opportunities are often offered. But we're neither owed nor promised multiple chances.

Another of the devil's favorites asserts: "Go with the crowd. There's safety in numbers. That many people couldn't be wrong." Think of the ten spies who opposed Joshua and Caleb and the generation that died as they followed the majority into unbelief. Think of the majority who hated Jeremiah as he spoke God's truth to ancient Israel. Think of the fickle crowds that first welcomed Jesus to Jerusalem and then demanded His death. Think of Matthew 7:13–14.

The older I get, the more I appreciate people you don't need to count behind. Not only can you trust their math, you can trust their hearts. We love such people and their godly values, but we love the God behind those values even more. God never hedges or miscalculates.

It's Like Grits

But the hour is coming, and now is, when the true worshipers will worship the Father in spirit and truth; for the Father is seeking such to worship Him. God is Spirit, and those who worship Him must worship in spirit and truth.

John 4:23–24

When I didn't recognize the word "polenta" on the school lunch menu, I asked about it. The response was, "It's like grits." Cool with me, as I've always been okay with grits. Turns out that opinions and judgments vary. It wasn't like grits; it was like cream of wheat. In my world, cream of wheat was invented to punish prisoners when they've been really bad. The meal fell notably short of my expectations.

It won't surprise you that others loved the meal. They found it unique, creative, and refreshing. Obviously, my palate is not so refined.

I wonder how much my expectations flavored my poor dining experience. We build mental pictures of anticipated experiences. As we do, feelings get attached to those pictures. When the experience falls short, our hearts hurt for what could have been.

Recently some friends attended a professional workshop. They read the brochure and expected an engaging and informative hands-on experience. What they got was a day of weird lecture that seemed to last a week. There was major disappointment in dashed expectations.

We sometimes face similar challenges with worship or Bible class. We think we know what we need. We're certain that we know what we want. But the experience doesn't match expectations. The experience falls short, and our hearts hurt for what could have been. Thankfully, we're not powerless in such situations. There are concrete, time-honored actions we can take. *We can evaluate our understanding of worship.* Is worship paying homage to God, or is it meeting my perceived needs? Worship certainly meets many of our needs (fellowship, encouragement, instruction, and admonishment), but love and devotion to God must be the heart of worship. We're blessed to focus upward first, outward second, and inward third during worship (John 4:23–24).

- *We can ask God to shape our hearts and open our minds to greater spiritual experience in worship.* If we come prepared for spiritual insight and connection, we're far more likely to achieve it (Psa 19:14).

- *We can set our minds on giving in worship—giving our attention and devotion to God, and giving encouragement to others.* See Luke 6:38 and Acts 20:35.

- *We can target one or more fellow Christians who seem to be struggling and bless them with extra attention before and after the worship assembly.* We can pray for them daily and be a purposeful conduit of God's grace for them (Heb 10:24).

- *We can remember that sermons and classes reach the ears and hearts of many people.* A lesson that doesn't speak as powerfully to me can be just what someone else needs. We can choose to be big-hearted.

- *We can even choose to supplement sermons and classes with our private study.* It takes work, but we're free and able to hear a sermon or a class on a higher level than it is presented. Please do this every time I preach or teach.

Small Treasures

And remember the words of the Lord Jesus, that He said, "It is more blessed to give than to receive."

Acts 20:35

I love books. I love bargains. I really love bargain books. Laura and I regularly plunder the discount carts at Books-A-Million, the bin at Big Lots, and the bookstore at the public library. Occasionally, we find offbeat treasures that help keep us out of trouble. Who could pass up *A Brief History of Rudeness, The Trouble with Perfect: How Parents Can Avoid the Overachievement Trap and Still Raise Successful Children,* or *Everything You Always Wanted to Know About God?* (No, it didn't tell me everything I always wanted to know, but it sure made me think!)

Sometimes we find books for us, but more often we find small treasures that fit the needs of the Overton Memorial Library. We love finding those small treasures. And we've learned to enjoy giving them away.

Learning to enjoy giving books away was a challenging lesson for me. I used to greatly enjoy keeping them. I was like Linus with his blanket. Books were comforting. They're low maintenance, they don't talk unless you want to listen, and they stay where you put them. They'll wait for you. Sometimes you just feel smarter for having them around.

On the flip side, books are heavy, they take up bunches of space, and they do no good unless you read them. I was very slow to realize that there's greater joy in sharing good books than in hoarding them. I hope I'm realizing that's true of more than just books.

Our culture is afflicted with the love of having. Think of the proliferation of self-storage units. I know some people put them to good and wise use. I fear that others pay good money to store things that will decay while waiting to be used. I fear that people sometimes feel trapped by those items, realizing that they'd feel a sense of loss without them (1 Tim 6:9–10, 17).

We need to pay more attention to Luke 12:15, "Take heed and beware of covetousness, for one's life does not consist in the abundance of the things he possesses." We need to pay more attention to 1 Timothy 6:6–7, "Now godliness with contentment is great gain. For we brought nothing into this world, and it is certain that we can carry nothing out."

We need to pay more attention to Matthew 6:19–21. Treasures on earth never last, but the treasures we send ahead to heaven honor God. Sending treasures ahead reduces both risk and stress. Having isn't nearly as rewarding as giving. The memory of giving takes up no space, requires no maintenance, and can be relived as often as needed or desired. And what seems a small treasure to the giver may be life-changing in the heart of the recipient. On top of that, gracious givers grow toward God (Jam 1:17–18).

It Don't Matter

For He says: "In an acceptable time I have heard you, and in the day of salvation I have helped you."

2 Corinthians 6:2

It's bad grammar, but excellent marketing. There's a restaurant on highway 331 in Highland Home, Alabama, called It Don't Matter. It's my assumption that this restaurant has positioned itself as the "default setting" for indecisive diners. She asks, "Where we eatin' at?" He replies, "It don't matter." Problem solved. Indecision "magically" becomes decision. Wouldn't it be nice if parts of life really worked that way? It might in some insignificant areas, but it could never work within the sphere of faith.

We all remember Joshua's farewell address. The most famous of his statements is Joshua 24:15, "Choose for yourselves this day whom you will serve, whether the gods which your fathers served on the other side of the River, or the gods of the Amorites, in whose land you dwell. But as for me and my house, we will serve the Lord."

We love Joshua's challenge. You can't have it both ways—it's God or the gods. You can't not choose. Failing to choose God is rejecting Him. So is choosing both God and the gods. The number one command from Sinai was, "You shall have no other gods before Me" (Exod 20:3). It's not that God gave permission for other gods to be secondary. Jesus' quotation of Deuteronomy 6:13 is, "You shall worship the Lord your God, and Him only you shall serve" (Matt 4:10). We remember Jesus' words from Matthew 6:24, "No one can serve two masters, for either he will hate the one and love the other, or else he will be loyal to the one and despise the other."

Elijah issued a challenge much like Joshua's. On Mount Carmel before his contest with hundreds of false prophets, Elijah said to the people, "How long will you falter between two opinions? If the Lord is God, follow Him; but if Baal, follow him." Unlike the people of Joshua's day who affirmed their faith in the Lord, 1 Kings 18:21 ends with this sad sentence: "But the people answered him not a word." They wouldn't choose until they saw how the contest ended. They walked by sight and not by faith.

When it comes to faith in the God of the Bible, "It don't matter" is bad grammar and worse theology. Jesus identified the first and great commandment, "You shall love the Lord your God with all your heart, with all your soul, and with all your mind" (Matt 22:37; Deut 6:5). Revelation 3:15–16 graphically reinforces the point, "I know your works, that you are neither cold nor hot. I could wish you were cold or hot. So then, because you are lukewarm, and neither cold nor hot, I will vomit you out of My mouth."

Loving God matters. Loving truth matters. Loving the church matters. Loving souls matters. Obeying God matters. Doing truth matters. Being in Christ matters. Being salt and light matters. In matters of the faith, "It don't matter" is the devil's own lie.

Live and Learn

Also do not take to heart everything people say, lest you hear your servant cursing you. For many times, also, your own heart has known that even you have cursed others.

Ecclesiastes 7:21–22

After many years of schooling and working with the public, I'm supposed to know something about communication. Lately, I've been reminded—again—of just how little I know.

Words sometimes strike us in fragile moments. What would have been harmless, or even well-received under normal circumstances, doesn't always find us receptive under such circumstances. Sometimes we're fragile because life has recently dealt us several blows. The cumulative effect of those blows has created a sore spot in our hearts. It has biased our thinking in a most negative way. Sometimes we're fragile because we have let our expectations soar; we're poised for an exceptional victory—but others don't know that, and they don't have any way to know that their words are letting us down (Eccl 7:21–22).

Words sometimes strike us in thoughtless moments. Our brains aren't in gear. Or maybe our brains are locked into the wrong gear. We hear the words in our unique, individual context, a perspective never imagined by the speaker. We don't really hear; we mis-hear. And we're shocked at the speaker's thoughtlessness, never realizing that we are the ones being thoughtless (Luke 8:18).

Words sometimes strike us in mean moments. We're already frustrated or hurting, and we've had enough. We're primed to pounce on the next "offender" who crosses our path. In our mean moments, we fail to hear with grace or mercy. We rush to judgment without considering that the supposed offender may have had the best of intentions (Eccl 7:8–9).

Thankfully, words sometimes strike us in gracious moments. We are acutely conscious of God's presence. His word is in our hearts, and our thoughts are aligned with His. On such occasions, we hear like God hears. We hear through wise and loving ears. We give people credit for meaning more than they are able to express. We remember that words don't always come out right. We choose to extend what we so often need, the benefit of the doubt (Prov 15:1; Eccl 7:5).

God is honored in such moments. Faith and friendship are strengthened in such moments. With God's help, we live and learn. To God be the glory for extending such grace to us all.

Deniers

Therefore whoever confesses Me before men, him I will also confess before My Father who is in heaven. But whoever denies Me before men, him I will also deny before My Father who is in heaven.

Matthew 10:32–33

Is there any fact of history so well established that no one attempts to deny it? Sadly, apparently not. Consider the following. There are people who deny that the search for religious freedom was a factor in the settlement of colonies that eventually became the United States of America. There are people who deny the Holocaust. My own family isn't immune. One of my grandfathers died still believing that humans never landed on the moon. He was certain that the lunar landing was staged for television in the Arizona desert. And one of the more recent examples is the controversy over the NBC News interviews with a man who denies the Sandy Hook Elementary School massacre of 2012. His inexplicable belief seems to be that the victims were just actors.

As you might gather, I am not among the deniers in the cases mentioned above. While I wasn't eyewitness to any of these events, I find the evidence for them compelling. I also find the fact that deniers persist to be unsurprising. People have an amazing ability to deny the challenging and the inconvenient. Deniers can be stunningly creative.

Consider the example from Jesus' ministry as recorded in Matthew 9:32–34. Evidently, His critics could not deny the reality of the exorcism that He effected. The possessed man was mute, but he spoke once the demon left. The multitudes knew what they had seen and were amazed. Still the deniers of Jesus' divinity had an answer: "He casts out demons by the ruler of the demons." Yes, He has power, but it's not godly power. We won't believe, no matter what we see. Evidently the Pharisees thought this tactic effective as they employed it again in Matthew 12:24.

Consider the example from Matthew 12:9–21. There's no dispute within the text that Jesus healed the man whose hand was withered. The issue here is that He effected the healing on the Sabbath, thus breaking one of the Pharisees' rules by working that day. Instead of celebrating the healing, the critics "went out and plotted against Him, how they might destroy Him." Tacitly, they denied both the goodness of Jesus and the goodness of His healing action.

A scarier example is found in Matthew 16:13–28. Just six verses after Peter's praiseworthy affirmation, "You are the Christ, the Son of the living God," Peter begins to rebuke the Lord. Peter denies Jesus' statement from Matthew 16:21 because it did not fit his understanding of the Messiah and His kingdom. Denial is not limited to those who don't know Jesus.

Denial also isn't limited to just our words. Titus 1:16 asserts, "They profess to know God, but in works they deny Him." Connect that with 2 Timothy 3:5's description of those who have "a form of godliness" but deny its power, and we're challenged to look inward and upward. If we don't live like Jesus taught and lived, we, too, are deniers of God's greatest act. We must never deny Christ or truth because, in the end, deniers get denied (Matt 7:21–23 and 10:32–33).

Stuck in My Head

I will meditate on Your precepts, and contemplate Your ways. I will delight myself in Your statutes; I will not forget Your word.

Psalm 119:15–16

I know my thinking is often odd, and that does not trouble me. I'm not sure I'm diagnosable, but that wouldn't bother me either. Ever get a song stuck in your head? Today it's A *Horse with No Name*. No clue why, but I've reached the point of recognizing my questions:

- Which desert?

- Why is he riding through it?

- If the horse being nameless is an issue, why not name him? Bob or Pete or Roadie.

I find myself wanting to replace lyrics. If the horse is a mare, I'd go with "riding through the desert on a horse named Loraine." Practically, I'd go with "riding through the desert on a horse is insane." Why a horse and not a camel? Could it be that "camel" is a harder rhyme? If the horse were hair-impaired, I'd try "riding through the desert on a horse with no mane." It gets worse, but I'll stop. I've not yet found a way to turn the song off or to replace it.

There is another set of questions:

- Wouldn't I be better off with a psalm, hymn, or Scripture stuck in my head?

- Is there a way to do that?

- Why is my impulse to write about this so persistent?

If I were smarter, wiser, or more spiritual, I wonder what would be stuck in my head? A leading candidate would be the famous words from the Psalms: "From everlasting to everlasting, You are God." Talk about a concept worth contemplating!

In Psalm 90, the idea is that God has always "been our dwelling place." We've never existed without Him. We couldn't exist without Him. He's from before the mountains or the seas, and He will still be here when they are gone. If we want to last, then God is our answer.

In Psalm 103:17, we are reminded, "But the mercy of the Lord is from everlasting to everlasting on those who fear Him." Endless mercy coupled with righteousness, love, protection, and care. He knows our need and our unworthiness, but He keeps showing mercy to all who will allow.

In Psalm 41:13 and 106:48 the idea is, "Blessed be the Lord God of Israel from everlasting to everlasting! And let all the people say amen." He's everlastingly holy, everlastingly worthy, and everlastingly honorable. If we could praise and bless Him forever, it still wouldn't be enough. There would still be new depths to discover and new heights to reach.

My mind can't grasp "everlasting," and I find that very comforting. The everlasting God is a God worth seeking. The everlasting God is a God worth knowing. The everlasting God can take us places and show us things that we'd never touch without Him. He has the time, but that's just the hem of the garment. He also has the knowledge, wisdom, power, and love. I need to have Him stuck in my head and heart full-time.

Language, Reality, and Humility

For I am the least of the apostles, who am not worthy to be called an apostle, because I persecuted the church of God.

1 Corinthians 15:9

I enjoy word games, especially those that are unexpected and accidental. Sometimes I enjoy them even when I'm the victim.

At times, I fill in for speakers who get sick, double-booked, or otherwise can't keep an appointment. In that role, introductions can be challenging.

- "Our scheduled speaker could not be here today," so I was the unscheduled speaker.

- "Our regular speaker could not be here today," so I was the irregular speaker.

- I really liked the double-up when the introduction began, "Our regularly scheduled speaker could not be here today...." I seldom get to be both irregular and unscheduled. I felt like I was multitasking.

- "Our announced speaker could not be here today," so I was the unannounced speaker, at least until the guy making the announcements announced me.

- "Our real speaker could not be here today," so I was the unreal speaker. I like that.

- "Our normal speaker could not be here today," so I got to be myself—happily abnormal.

- I won't use real names to protect everyone, but on one occasion it was, "As you know, we had brother _____ scheduled for today. When he couldn't come, we tried brothers _____, _____, and _____, but they couldn't come either. So, our speaker for today is Bill Bagents." You know what they say—when you get to the bottom of the barrel, something is there. And one friend (frenemy?) began his introduction: "We thought about getting a preacher to speak for our Teacher Appreciation Banquet tonight, but we thought you'd enjoy hearing Bill instead." I'm not sure why, but it's okay being a non-preaching preacher.

It's good not to take offense, especially when none is being offered. It's good to see the humor and to learn from it. Those who stand on ceremony are certain to suffer the occasional stunningly unceremonious fall. There's no blessing, and great danger, in thinking more highly of ourselves than we ought to think (Rom 12:3).

Even if offense is being offered, we don't have to accept the offer. Think of the praise Peter heaps on Jesus, "who, when He was reviled, did not revile in return; when He suffered, He did not threaten, but committed Himself to Him who judges righteously" (1 Pet 2:23). Remember the principle taught in Ecclesiastes 7:21. "Also do not take to heart everything that people say, lest you hear your servant cursing you." Some words are best ignored and forgotten.

I like people who are pleasant, good-natured, extra generous, and hard to offend. I want to follow their example. We need to follow their example. They are peacemakers and peace seekers—true children of God (Matt 5:9; Rom 12:18; Heb 12:14; 1 Pet 3:11).

Consistency

And He who sent Me is with Me. The Father has not left Me alone, for I always do those things that please Him.

John 8:29

I'm never quite sure how to phrase it. Is it that I love consistency or that I hate inconsistency?

My brother has a tractor that won't behave consistently. Its electrical issue is intermittent—it acts up only when it wants to. He'd take it to the shop, but he knows what would happen. It would never mess up while the mechanic was watching.

On the positive side, we love a restaurant that's consistent. A given dish comes out the same every time. The price is uniform. The service is always friendly. If I have to ask, "Is the salmon good today?" I have already admitted defeat.

We love Hebrews 13:8, "Jesus Christ is the same yesterday, today, and forever." It's the perfect affirmation of consistency. Lest we miss that point, the very next verse urges us to be consistent in our faith, "established" and not "carried about by various and strange doctrines."

There are many ways we can show consistency in Christ.

- We can worship consistently with faith and passion (Heb 10:24–25; 13:15).

- We can consistently show God's love to others (Heb 13:16; Gal 6:10).

- We can consistently value and add to our knowledge of God's word (Acts 17:11; 2 Tim 2:15).

- We can consistently do good works that bring glory to God (Matt 5:16; Titus 3:1).

- We can consistently show respect for God's authority (Col 3:17; 1 Pet 5:6).

- We can consistently encourage good works and good people (Eph 4:29; Gal 6:6).

- We can consistently pray for God's will to be honored (1 Thess 5:17; 1 Tim 2:1–4).

- We can consistently confess our sins and seek God's forgiveness (1 John 2:1–2; Jam 5:16).

- We can consistently "give all diligence" to grow in Christ (2 Pet 1:5–8, 12–13).

- We can consistently "esteem others better" than ourselves and "look out for ... the interests of others" (Phil 2:3–4).

Using Scripture to add to this list could fill weeks of happy Bible study. The amazing gracious and loving consistency of our God urges us to spiritual consistency. Ephesians 4:11–16 beautifully states our goal. We want to be fully and completely like Christ.

Doublespeak

Woe to you, blind guides, who say, "Whoever swears by the temple, it is nothing; but whoever swears by the gold of the temple, he is obliged to perform it." Fools and blind! For which is greater, the gold or the temple that sanctifies the gold?

Matthew 23:16–17

I detest doublespeak. So does Jesus, as per Matthew 5:33–37, 15:1–9, and 23:16–22. Jesus opposed both the verbal variety and the doublespeak where one's actions contradict his words.

There's nothing clean, clear, or Christian about doublespeak. Modern examples abound.

- "Please accept our free product; just pay shipping and handling." "Free" never demands payment.

- "New, lower price," but the size of the box decreased more than its cost. Under the new approach, you pay more per ounce of product.

- An advertisement for a book claimed that it was both "recently published" and "forthcoming." Unless they have discovered time travel, one of those is wrong.

- A news anchor declared a product "always usually effective." I know that's better than "always usually mostly effective." But please pick one. Please pick the one that's true.

- The contractor promises, "I'll be there on Thursday at 8:00 sharp," knowing that he has made that same promise to two other clients.

Doublespeak can be a bit humorous when the stakes are low or if it doesn't directly impact us. Usually, it's highly annoying. It destroys trust. It damages relationships and reputations. We avoid it in faithful consideration of Matthew 5:37, Ephesians 4:25, and Revelation 21:8.

The religious versions of doublespeak are far worse than anything mentioned above.

- "If we say we have fellowship with Him, and walk in darkness, we lie and do not practice the truth" (1 John 1:6).

- "If we say we have not sinned, we make Him a liar, and His word is not in us" (1 John 1:10).

- "He who says, 'I know Him,' and does not keep His commandments is a liar and the truth is not in him" (1 John 2:4).

- "He who says he is in the light and hates his brother, is in the darkness until now" (1 John 2:9). Also consider 1 John 4:7–21, especially verse 20.

- "My little children, let us not love in word or tongue, but in deed and in truth" (1 John 3:18). Combined with 3:16–17 and James 2:14–18, we clearly see the danger of spiritual doublespeak. There's no virtue in it. It's an insult to both God and man.

Captain Obvious

Then he who had received the one talent came and said, "Lord, I knew you to be a hard man, reaping where you have not sown, and gathering where you have not scattered seed. And I was afraid, and went and hid your talent in the ground. Look, there you have what is yours."

Matthew 25:24–25

Some things seem too obvious to merit even a mention. For instance, a recent headline stated, "Rolling Roadblock May Cause Traffic Delays." Troopers were planning to "pace" interstate traffic in order to enhance safety in a roadwork zone. I can promise that delays were caused. Here are a few other examples:

- A pet food can stating, "Not for human consumption." I thought "pet food" covered that.

- "Do not take _____ (you pick the name of the medicine) if you are allergic to _____ or any of its ingredients." How would you know you're allergic to anything before you've been exposed to it? Intuition?

- "Do not feed the bears." I'm pretty sure that it's not wise to feed any animal in the wild that sees you as food. The bear may not be through eating when you think you're through feeding him.

- Medicine bottle label: "Take only as prescribed." You think? Does anyone think that just possessing the pills without ingesting them could help? Maybe some think they'd get well faster if they took all the pills on day one.

We know why such warnings get printed. Corporate lawyers want to limit liability. If there's a way to misunderstand or misuse anything, someone will find it. Humans are infamous for failing to use the brains that God gave us.

These observations cause me to consider similar stunningly dumb statements from Scripture. Even there we read things that never should have been thought or said. We know God accurately reports such statements to warn us to think before we speak and act.

- "The woman whom You gave to be with me, she gave me of the tree, and I ate" (Gen 3:12). Blaming. Excuse-making. Attempting to pass the buck. Never has worked, and never will work.

- "Am I my brother's keeper?" (Gen 4:9). It was a functional lie and an attempt to deny familial obligation.

- "Come, let us build ourselves a city and a tower whose top is in the heavens; let us make a name for ourselves" (Gen 11:4). Ignore God in making plans. See how well that works out.

- "Look, this dreamer is coming! Come therefore, let us now kill him and cast him into some pit" (Gen 37:19–20). They were talking about their own brother!

A Burn, Two Blisters, and a Cut

And when her mourning was over, David sent and brought her to his house, and she became his wife and bore him a son. But the thing that David had done displeased the Lord.

2 Samuel 11:27

Some recent weekend work left my hands a bit damaged—a burn, two blisters, and a cut. If left uncovered to heal, they looked bad. If covered with bandages, they invited many questions. All four wounds looked worse than they were. All four healed completely in time.

People were both kind and curious about the wounds. As they noticed, they either asked about them or offered some comment. I still appreciate their concern.

Wounds that we can see are the easy ones. It's acceptable to ask about them and to express concern. Unseen wounds are a different, much more complicated matter.

I wonder if Abram knew the level of Lot's error when "he pitched his tent even as far as Sodom" (Gen 13:12). Because we know the story, we see the phrase as ominous foreshadowing. The next verse demands that we do. It's hard to do right and be right when surrounded by people who are "exceedingly wicked and sinful against the Lord." Sometimes we can see the peril, but we're helpless to stop the chain of events.

I wonder if Abram could sense the danger when Sarai offered him her servant as a concubine (Gen 16). God's plan of one man married to one woman for life had been clear from the beginning (Gen 2). Human attempts to "help God out" often end in pain. The plan upset the dynamics of their camp. When Hagar "had conceived, her mistress became despised in her eyes" (Gen 16:4).

Sarai blamed Abram for the wound (Gen 16:5), and the level of pain deepened.

I wonder how Leah found the heart to cope with her wound of being first wife, but second choice, to Jacob (Gen 29ff.). Rachel felt envy because Leah had children while she did not (Gen 30:1). Her envy led to demands that Jacob could not meet, to frustration, and to anger. It led Rachel to repeat the same error that Sarai made. It set the stage for favoritism, rivalry, deceit, and years of remorse. Sin exacts awful costs. The way of the transgressor has always been difficult (Prov 13:15).

I wonder if Ishmael ever healed from being sent away by Abraham (Gen 21). Not just sent away but imperiled in the Wilderness of Beersheba. Yes, God heard his cries (Gen 21:17) and sent an angel to intervene. Yes, God promised to make Ishmael a great nation (Gen 21:18). But trauma runs deep, and its effects are often hidden. Unseen wounds are often the cruelest.

I wonder if the Egyptians around Joseph could sense his sadness. Sold as a slave by his brothers, knowing that he would have been killed except for Reuben's kindness and the providence of God (Gen 37). I wonder if Jacob realized how his parental favoritism contributed to this sorry situation. Day after day, his remaining sons saw his abject grief (Gen 37:34–35). How maintaining their lie must have weighed on their hearts (Gen 42:21–22)!

I wonder if David had a clue about the depth and duration of Nathan's words from 2 Samuel 12:10, "The sword shall never depart from your house, because you have despised Me." Rape, murder, treason, and civil war. Atrocity upon atrocity because of a cycle of sin that began in one selfish act. And David surely knew that it was a self-inflicted wound. Do we know, too?

Outcomes

But what do you think? A man had two sons, and he came to the first and said, "Son, go, work today in my vineyard." He answered and said, "I will not," but afterward he regretted it and went. Then he came to the second and said likewise. And he answered and said, "I go, sir," but he did not go.

Matthew 21:28–30

For an ever-increasing number of people, it's not music unless it makes the earth shake. I prefer a volume that doesn't make my teeth hurt.

Some like hummus, sushi, and tofu. I'd rather not eat than eat sushi. I couldn't spell "hummus" without help.

Some think of squirrels as cute and funny little creatures. To me, they're rats with bushy tails.

I recently saw an internet story that anyone could love. A group of teens shared dinner and enjoyed the experience. Upon reflection, they realized the tip they left was embarrassingly low. They sent the waiter a touching and well-written note of apology and appreciation. The note included enough money to raise their tip to 18%. How cool is that!

In many situations we get only one bite at the apple. What we do in that moment stands or falls forever. We can learn from it for next time, but we can't change the outcome.

In other situations, we can improve the outcome if we're willing. I love the example of those teens:

- If it doesn't feel right, explore the reasons.

- Don't be afraid to ask yourself challenging questions.

- Seek counsel to maximize understanding and to identify options for improvement.

- Don't settle.

- Don't excuse.

- Don't rationalize.

- Step up. As you learn better, do better.

- Whenever it's possible, turn a negative into a positive.

How do you think the teens felt when the waiter shared their note and it went viral? I'd be WOWED. I hope they realize how their repentance (if I can use the biblical word) set such a fine example for others. It speaks of heart, intelligence, and responsibility.

I love the waiter's choice to share the letter. It contained no names, so there was no violation of privacy. I see it as his grateful response to their gracious action—a win/win situation where everybody chose to do right.

So much of life seems dominated by zero-sum thinking. If I win, you lose. It's a pleasure to see thinking and action on a higher level. That makes me think of God, godliness, and God's word.

- "Therefore, as we have opportunity, let us do good to all" (Gal 6:10).

- "For the fruit of the Spirit is in all goodness, righteousness, and truth" (Eph 5:9).

- "Therefore, as the elect of God, holy and beloved, put on tender mercies, kindness, meekness, longsuffering" (Col 3:12).

When we see a great example, we're blessed to follow it. What outcomes do I need to change? What behaviors do I need to improve? What God-honoring actions should I take today?

Sweet Phrases

Let the words of my mouth and the meditation of my heart be acceptable in Your sight, O Lord, my strength and my Redeemer.

Psalm 19:14

"Let your speech always be with grace, seasoned with salt, that you may know how you ought to answer each one" (Col 4:6). "The mouth of the righteous is a well of life" (Prov 10:11). "The tongue of the righteous is choice silver" (Prov 10:20). "A word fitly spoken is like apples of gold in settings of silver" (Prov 25:11). "A fool vents all his feelings, but a wise man holds them back" (Prov 29:11).

I recently asked a friend at work, "What is Leo (pseudonym) doing now?" Her sweet reply was, "I think he works fulltime at taking care of himself." I know what she meant and appreciated her effort to be nice. Sometimes life gangs up on people, and they don't recover. Just getting through each day becomes a fulltime job. Others of us just can't get out of our own way.

Another friend was asked, "What kind of worker is Clyde (another pseudonym)?" The answer was, "He tries really hard." Again, I saw this as a major attempt to be kind. It was also a major effort to avoid being condemning while remaining ethical. Nothing good comes of a lie, but much good comes from a gracious, gentle response.

The owner of a new and very ugly hat loved her hat. She kept asking people, "Isn't my new hat pretty?" The perfect reply from a friend was, "I'm so glad you like it!" Validation without dishonesty—how wise. It shows great maturity to resist unleashing a zinger in the face of such tailormade temptation.

A friend was asked his opinion of an applicant for an important job. He responded, "I believe you'd be blessed to look further." In a similar circumstance another friend said, "I don't really think this job fits his skillset." Again, we love the non-acer-bic honesty. There's no intent to harm, just effort to be truthful and maintain integrity.

Being a southerner, I recognize the grace and utility of "Bless his/her heart." Depending on context, the meaning can range from "If I didn't have a healthy respect for God, I'd shoot you where you stand" to "I'd love to help you, but I haven't a clue how to try."

Being Christian, we recognize that certain biblical phrases (and sentences) always stand ready to bless us and those whom we need to help.

- "God is love" (1 John 4:8, 16).

- "We love Him because He first loved us" (1 John 4:19).

- "Love never fails" (1 Cor 13:8).

- "I will never leave you nor forsake you" (Heb 13:5; Deut 31:6, 8).

- "This hope we have as an anchor of the soul, both sure and steadfast" (Heb 6:19).

- "Therefore He is able to save to the uttermost" (Heb 7:25).

- "If God is for us, who can be against us?" (Rom 8:31)

Time and Flow

*To everything there is a season, a time for every purpose un-
der heaven.*

Ecclesiastes 3:1

A recent visit to the farm reminded me of the importance of time and flow. My brothers were rolling hay as the summer showers allowed. Timeliness demanded that the hay be cut—if it gets too large, it gets "stemmy" and it falls over. Once cut, it has to dry sufficiently before it can be rolled. If rolled too green, it will decay or combust—neither is a desirable option.

If the grass cut for hay is really thick, it will need to be "fluffed" (aka tedded) to help it dry in a timely fashion. As things would have it, a bearing failed on the tedder, and a new one wouldn't arrive until after the weekend. So you wait.

I asked my dad about their goal for the number of rolls of hay. His answer is always the same: "They put up hay like there will be no winter grazing, and they plant winter grazing like there will be no hay. If you do both, it usually works out."

The hay equipment is big enough and sufficiently expensive that I don't even offer to help. Machines and I have a poor history—think of wheels falling off, engine problems, and major operator error. The big German cutter handles 32 feet in a swath. My brother, Randy, does things with the bailer that I'd have to think about way too long and still would do incorrectly. When everything is working, it's one more smooth operation.

Their harvesting of hay is like so much of life. It can't be rushed. If the Lord sends rain, you wait. If the equipment breaks, you wait. You can wait happily, angrily, or anywhere in between, but you still wait. If you do all you can when you can, the result tends to be okay.

Of course the Bible speaks to time and flow. Perhaps we think first of Ecclesiastes 3: "To everything there is a season, a time for every purpose under heaven," including "a time to plant and a time to pluck." There's also James 5:7: "Therefore be patient, brethren, until the coming of the Lord. See how the farmer waits for the precious fruit of the earth, waiting patiently for it until it receives the early and latter rain." That's a powerful reminder of time and flow. It's an invitation to trust God to run His universe and His world as He knows best.

In fact, God will run His universe and His world as He knows best. (We know that certain aspects run horribly awry because God allows an amazing degree of freedom to humans.) We also know that when we align our hearts and wills with God, the time and flow of life work so much better. We can huff, puff, and push with little to show for all the stress. Or we can choose to "wait upon the Lord" (Isa 40:27–31). We can choose to delight in the Lord, trusting Him to give us the desires of our hearts (Psa 37:4).

We know the adage, "Good things come to him who waits." It would be far more accurate to say, "Good things come to those who wait **on the Lord** and work hard while they wait." There's a lot to say for respecting the time and flow God has built into His world. Without that respect, there is endless pain and frustration.

Communication Glitches

Even things without life, whether flute or harp, when they make a sound, unless they make a distinction in the sounds, how will it be known what is piped or played? For if the trumpet makes an uncertain sound, who will prepare for battle?

1 Corinthians 14:7–8

I can't remember where I first read, "Communication is an art; become an artist." I love the sentiment, but I've never been able to live up to it.

I asked how a meeting went. The response was, "It went better than I expected." I think that's good, but it's impossible to be certain. Could be that the expectation was a firing, but there was only a lay-off. Could be the expectation was a $20,000 cost, but the cost was only $10,000. "Better than I expected" doesn't always mean good or desirable.

People often say in winter, "It sure is cold outside." My usual response is, "Yes, it's great" or some version thereof. I'm fine with the cold. Most of the people initiating the comment aren't. I've been accused of "messing with them." I won't deny that, but I'm also having fun and embracing reality.

Being sometimes known as a counselor, I have communication issues with, "How are you?" About 99 times out of 100, I mean that in the polite, generic, and not intrusive sense. It amazes me how many people hear it differently. I'm learning to respect their right to do so. If it blesses you to tell me how you REALLY are, I'm happy to listen.

We dine at a local Mexican restaurant most Sundays. Frequently, I eat the shrimp and rice without the rice. That saves a bunch of carbs, but it sounds funny. It's not as bad as Laura ordering the duck and sausage pasta (at the Italian place), "minus the duck." Our ticket records the order as "duck, no duck."

We can unintentionally cause communication glitches. Most recently, we killed a cash register at a local bookstore. The keyboard just quit talking to the computer. We weren't at all surprised.

Major experience with communication glitches has strong educational value. We've learned:

- *Never assume that things are perfectly clear.* Perfect is exceedingly rare in this world. Clarity and understanding are not too frequent, either. Even Jesus was misunderstood.

- *Learn to laugh at communication glitches.* Laughing beats crying, fussing, fuming, and blaming.

- *God sets us a great example with the frequent repetition in Scripture.* Multiple hearings can minimize misunderstanding.

- *The more tired, stressed, or rushed we are, the more frequent the communication glitches.* And those factors also make the glitches that occur seem worse. Self-control and patience are MAJOR virtues.

- *The Bible is a masterpiece on communication.* Think of Matthew 5:37, Ephesians 4:29–32, and Colossians 4:5–6. Everything works better when those teachings are employed.

- *God is the Master Communicator.* Nothing surpasses seeking to understand Him.

Delete Forever

No more shall every man teach his neighbor, and every man his brother, saying, "Know the Lord," for they all shall know Me, from the least of them to the greatest of them, says the Lord. For I will forgive their iniquity, and their sin I will remember no more.

Jeremiah 31:34

Generally speaking, I like getting email. Loads of interesting and informative items come my way. Of course there's also some junk. When I know an email is junk, my favorite option becomes "delete forever." When I click on that box, I'm done.

My tech savvy friends remind me that "delete forever" is just an illusion. They tell me that even things I delete can be found and recovered by people who know how. I wish I didn't believe them. It would be so much more pleasant to believe that "delete forever" means just what it says.

There's not much in life that works on a "delete forever" basis. From a few physical scars to some memories that I'd love to erase, experience tells me that consequences tend to hang around long after I wish they were gone. And it's good to know that. Preachers have often stated, "Sin will take you further than you want to go, keep you longer than you want to stay, and cost you more than you want to pay." Somehow, we know that is "scary true." Knowing that it's true should make us more prayerful and more careful. Implications are clear:

- Don't set in motion what you can't stop.

- Don't pretend that no one else will know.

- Don't pretend that no one else will be hurt.

- Don't pretend that even God's forgiveness removes all the consequences.

1 Samuel 12 and the events that follow stunningly support each of these truths. Had David known what sending for Bathsheba would eventually cost him, he'd never have initiated the sin.

As sure as I am that my "delete forever" button doesn't really do what it says, I'm so happy that God's does. While never denying the present-day consequences of sin, I love the following passages:

- "The Lord also has put away your sin, you shall not die" (2 Sam 12:13).

- "Purge me with hyssop, and I shall be clean. Wash me, and I shall be whiter than snow" (Psa 51:7).

- "For as the heavens are high above the earth, so great is His mercy toward those who fear Him. As far as east is from the west, so far has He removed our transgressions from us. As a father pities his children, so the Lord pities those who fear Him" (Psa 103:11–13).

- "Therefore He is able to save to the uttermost those who come to God through Him, since He always lives to make intercession for them" (Heb 7:25).

Temporal consequences are undeniable. Sin is never a light or laughing matter. But when God forgives a sin, "delete forever" still applies. The stunning truth of Jeremiah 31:34 is repeated in both Hebrews 8:12 and 10:17, "For I will forgive their iniquity, and their sin I will remember no more." What a promise! What a God!

Watcha Doin'?

Walk in wisdom toward those who are outside, redeeming the time. Let your speech always be with grace, seasoned with salt, that you may know how you ought to answer each one.

Colossians 4:5–6

Someone has been sending me a weekly "Watcha Doin'?" text message. Laura, my phone, and I don't recognize the number. Our theory is that someone is misdialing.

There's a part of me that wants to respond to the sender. I've thought about texting, "I don't think your message is reaching the correct party." But I've also thought about texting one of the following:

- "Trying to figure out who you are." That would be honest.

- "None of your business. I don't think I know you." But that sounds rude.

- "Who wants to know?" That seems a bit blunt.

- "Nothing." But that wouldn't be quite right. I'm almost always doing something. Part of me wonders if it's possible to be doing nothing. Even daydreaming and taking a break are doing something.

- "As little as I can." Sometimes that's way too true.

- "Just chillin'. What are you doing?" At least it's on the "reflective listening" side of life.

- "Sitting here with my wife." If the texter is "trolling," this might send an important "I'm unavailable" message.

- "Preparing my sermon for next Sunday." If they're up to no good, that might remind them that God is always watching. If they're reaching out for help, that might remind them that spiritual help is available.

- "Praying." Wouldn't that be appropriate in light of 1 Thessalonians 1:2–4, and 1 Timothy 2:1–7?

- "Studying my Bible." Often true, and certainly in keeping with Psalm 1 and 119.

- "Counting my blessings." That's such a match with 1 Thessalonians 5:16–18.

- "Contemplating the goodness of God." See Psalm 136 and Philippians 4:4–9. I know that the last five options trump the others hands down.

Look at the Ducks

The heavens declare the glory of God; and the firmament shows His handiwork.

Psalm 19:1

Recently, a formation of Canada Geese was honking away in the sky above town. There was just enough time to locate them and get a good view before they were gone. A grandmother was trying her best to get her grandson to notice, but the kid was on a toy-seeking mission. He never did look skyward. All the while his granny kept repeating, "Look at the ducks!"

Being a teacher, it took great restraint for me to keep my mouth shut, but I won that battle. The kid never saw the birds, so he wasn't being misled. The granny didn't know her honks from her quacks, but I can't see that damaging her. It's unlikely that a comment from me would have been helpful. Even I know that sometimes it's best just to keep walking.

Still, part of me laments the error and the loss of a teachable moment. Reflection continues even as I type these words.

- *It's natural for us to want to share information with others.* If it's natural in the broader sense, shouldn't it be essential in the realm of spiritual information? We should want to tell people what we know about God, Jesus, hope, joy, and peace.

- *It's natural for us to want to correct errors.* It's not judgmental or condescending to want to speak up for accuracy. There's something appealing about truth and off-putting about error. That tendency is especially important when it comes to biblical truth.

- *It's natural for us to focus on what we want in the moment.* Sometimes that focus helps us. With the little grandson, it robbed him of an opportunity to see something special. As the grandmother was urging him to look upward, the geese were changing the lead in their formation. One slipped back and another took over, just as smoothly as could be.

- *It's natural for us to think that what we "know" is correct.* I don't think the grandmother was attempting to deceive her grandson. She just wanted him to look at the flight of birds. She may not have known that she called the geese ducks. I can identify with her. Many times, I've been unaware of my errors that were stunningly obvious to others.

- *It's natural for us share special moments with those whom we love.* The grandmother saw and appreciated the birds. She wanted her grandson to join her in that moment. Seeing their disconnect was a bit sad. We can't tell people what they don't want to hear. We can't show people, even those we love, what they don't want to see.

- *It's natural for Christians to see the flight maneuvers of the geese and think of Psalm 19:1.* We interpret the skill, instinct, and beauty of the birds as demonstrations of God's glory. But a hunter might be thinking, "That could be dinner if I had my gun and they were in range." A motorist might think, "I hope they don't fly over my car and leave a mess." A pilot might think, "I hope they avoid the airport." For someone who either doesn't know or doesn't believe Psalm 19, there might be no thought of God at all. We don't want that option. Don't you wish God was always our first thought?

Outlook and Attitude

Trust in the Lord, and do good; dwell in the land, and feed on His faithfulness.

Psalm 37:3

O ne of the newer board members at Heritage Christian University set up an appointment for our VP of Advancement to meet with a church eldership. He not only arranged the appointment, he attended the meeting. We sent that board member a brief email of thanks. Here's what he sent back:

> *"So happy to be with him in this effort. I have been privileged to speak with a few elders in congregations near us and am waiting on them to get back with me. They are small congregations, but I do believe we will be getting a positive response from them. Thanks for giving me the opportunity to be a part."*

What an outlook and attitude! He's helping us try to bless the Lord's church in an unpaid position, and *he's* thanking *us* for letting him serve. So many Scriptures come to mind:

- "Let your light so shine before men, that they may see your good works, and glorify your Father in heaven" (Matt 5:16).

- "Render to all their due...honor to whom honor" (Rom 13:7).

- "Imitate me, just as I also imitate Christ" (1 Cor 11:1).

- "For they have refreshed my spirit and yours" (1 Cor 16:18).

- "He who sows bountifully will also reap bountifully" (2 Cor 9:6).

- "Brethren, join in following my example, and note those who so walk, as you have us for a pattern" (Phil 3:17).

- "And whatever you do, do it heartily, as to the Lord and not to men, knowing that from the Lord you will receive the reward of the inheritance; for you serve the Lord Christ" (Col 3:23–24).

- "In everything give thanks, for this is the will of God in Christ Jesus for you" (1 Thess 5:18).

- "But be an example to the believers in word, in conduct, in love, in spirit, in faith, in purity" (1 Tim 4:12).

- "Do good, that they be rich in good works, ready to give, willing to share" (1 Tim 6:18).

- "Be ready for every good work" (Titus 3:1).

Number Four

I returned and saw under the sun that—the race is not to the swift, nor the battle to the strong, nor bread to the wise, nor riches to men of understanding, nor favor to men of skill; but time and chance happen to them all.

Ecclesiastes 9:11

I enjoy watching several of the Olympic competitions. My favorites are those where each medalist seems elated to have succeeded at such a high level. I especially appreciate those who thank God, family, coaches, teammates, and supporters. It's encouraging when world class athletes remind us that they didn't reach that level alone, when they acknowledge those who helped them succeed.

My least favorite moments are just the opposite. They're the ones where the victors are "I, me, my" oriented. Selfishness and arrogance can taint most any occasion.

Among my oddities is a tendency to think about the athletes who finish number four, just off the medal stand. Sometimes it's just hundredths of a second or just a single point. On rare occasions, they even earn the same score as the bronze medalist, but the tie-breaking system bumps them to fourth. I wonder how they handle the disappointment of getting so close but falling short of major recognition.

We love to win. We love winners. We'd be blessed to remember that there's more to winning than the medal. I love those wise athletes who celebrate personal bests and maximum effort. There's something noble about giving your best. There's something noble about preparing like a champion. There's something noble about wanting to win.

I'm always encouraged by the fourth-place finisher who genuinely congratulates those who won the medals. We don't always win. We don't always meet our own expectations. It shows real class and wisdom to be happy for the success of others (Rom

12:15). Losing well can be a powerful way of winning on a higher level.

I'm always encouraged that God puts us in so many win-win situations. We don't take the "win at any cost" approach. Often, we excel only to the degree that we help others (Phil 2:1–4). Often, we excel only to the degree that we love others as God has loved us (Col 3:12–17; 1 John 4:7–11).

Sometimes being number four isn't such a bad thing. It may bring an opportunity to grow. It may bring an opportunity reflect. It may bring an opportunity to keep one's ego in check and to thank God that things are as good as they are.

Consider the Irises

But do not forget to do good and to share, for with such sac-rifices God is well pleased.

Hebrews 13:16

Laura's irises bloomed abundantly in three stages this spring. The vast majority, perhaps a hundred stems, were the deepest purple ever. The second phase was bright yellow, fewer in number but rich in beauty. Finally came the bronze. Bronze, if it comes, is always last.

Even though I grew up on a farm, we don't do so well with plants. We love the irises, because they thrive despite our lack of talent. We also love them because they came from the house in Huntsville where my wife grew up. They're a living connection to memories of South Plymouth Road.

Some three decades ago, we were blessed with a good idea. Collect some of the irises to transplant in Florence. And the Lord has taken care of them ever since. We still enjoy seeing and learning from these hardy plants. As the title above suggests, we're reminded of Matthew 6:28, "Consider the lilies of the field, how they grow."

- We're moved to think of Psalm 19:1–4, how nature declares the glory of God.

- We're reminded that no beauty rivals the simple beauty created by God. We can't improve on God's design (Matt 6:28–29).

- We think of how well God does when we don't get in His way.

- We're blessed to remember—in healthy ways—our connections to the past. Good times and rich blessings need to be preserved and treasured.

- We're reminded of the brevity of some forms of beauty. The iris blooms don't last long, but that's part of what makes them special. We focus on enjoying them rather than lamenting their swift departure (Psa 103:15; Isa 40:6–8).

- We look forward to the irises every spring. Some years there are few flowers, and all are purple. Some years, we get two colors, but seldom three. It's always a surprise. Sometimes, it's good not to know just how things are going to work out. It's good that we don't run the universe. It's better that we serve the Lord who does.

Laura's family now lives in rural Madison County in Alabama. Rumor is that one day we'll assist in transplanting some of the irises to their current lawns. I like that. Share and re-share, continue to appreciate pleasant parts of our past, and never forget God's blessings. That's good for our souls (Gal 6:9–10).

The Fundamental Flaw

As each one has received a gift, minister it to one another, as good stewards of the manifold grace of God.

1 Peter 4:10

The ongoing spate of airline service and public relations blunders amazes me. On one level, I'm surprised because my experience with a variety of airlines—mostly in traveling for mission trips—has been quite positive. On another level, I'm surprised in the sense of "what were they thinking?" There is no reality in which some of these events could possibly make sense.

For instance, a violinist trying to fly out of Houston was told that her seventeenth century violin would have to be checked as baggage. She inquired about other options and was told, if reports are correct, that there were no other options. She even suffered a slight injury as an airline employee tried to take her violin.

How crazy dumb sad is that? There's no way a fragile piece of history should be on a general purpose "wham and slam" conveyer belt. Trying to take the violin? Unimaginable. And there are always options, even if they're expensive or inconvenient.

Of course, I wasn't present to see this situation, but that doesn't keep me from wanting to learn from it. Assuming that the report is accurate, what went wrong? What was the fundamental flaw in the thinking and performance of the ticket agent and the supervisor who "assisted" her? Three possibilities immediately come to mind.

First, the—in my view—irrational airline employees could have just been following the rules. Any item exceeding a certain size must be checked. The violin exceeded that size; end of story. The violin gets checked. If that's the thinking, what a stunning example of the limitation of rules! Human rules are seldom inviolate. Special circumstances merit special consideration.

Second, the situation may have become a power struggle. "We're in charge here, we say what gets checked and what doesn't. Don't challenge our authority." If so, the employees need serious additional training. Don't go zero-sum, I win-you lose. Look for win-win alternatives.

It's possible the flaw in this depressing situation is even more fundamental. The violinist could have been dealing with individuals who just didn't care. "It's my way or the highway. Do as you are told. Check the violin, or you don't get on our plane." Not caring opens the door to all manner of abuses.

As Christians, we neither have nor want the option of not caring. We always represent Christ.

- From the creation, we recognize the fundamental dignity of every person created in the image of God (Gen 1:26–27).

- As Bible believers, we recognize the principles of love that undergird all of Scripture (Matt 22:36–40).

- We embrace God's Golden Rule (Matt 7:12).

- We look for ways to bless and encourage others (Eph 4:29; Phil 2:3–4).

- We acknowledge and welcome God's law of sowing and reaping, and our commission to "do good to all" (Gal 6:1–10).

- We actively pursue peace (Rom 12:18; 14:19).

If we don't, we let God down, and we look even worse than those foolish airline workers.

Dollars and Sense

For what profit is it to a man if he gains the whole world, and loses his own soul? Or what will a man give in exchange for his soul?

Matthew 16:26

I'm fundamentally anti-debt, but several recent articles have surprised me. An increasing number of college graduates are experiencing buyer's remorse. Student debt makes them wish they had never gone to college. Thinking in strictly economic terms, they have a point. A degree does not always equal a satisfying and lucrative career. A degree doesn't even guarantee a job. But what of the non-economic benefits? What of the friends made, the skills gained, broadening one's understanding of the world, and what of learning how to learn?

To change examples, we know what the tax assessor thinks our house is worth. We also know it's worth more than that to us because of the memories. Emotional factors may not be easy to quantify, but that doesn't make them less real. We value our house, but even that value is relative. If there were a fire, I'll be fine as long my wife is fine. The things, as important as some of them seem to be, are just things. The people always count first and most.

I'm amazed that some seem to assume that the value of everything can be measured in dollars and cents. I'm astounded that some Christians seem to share that view. Jesus didn't.

- Jesus promoted the value of one's soul above the material value of the whole world. "For what profit is it to a man if he gains the whole world, and is himself destroyed or lost?" (Luke 9:25).

- Jesus stated, "One's life does not consist in the abundance of things he possesses" (Luke 12:15).

- We all know how Jesus vividly contrasted the value of earthly vs. heavenly treasures (Matt 6:19–21).

The Bible as a whole does not support the idea of "everything has a price" or "everything can be measured in dollars and cents." "He who loves silver will not be satisfied with silver; nor he who loves abundance with increase" (Eccl 5:10). "For we brought nothing into this world, and it is certain that we can carry nothing out" (1 Tim 6:7). Paul emphasized how important it is for the "rich in this present age" to "be rich in good works" (1 Tim 6:17–19). "This present age" will end. There's more to come.

I guess it would be possible to put a dollar figure on the cost of my formal education. It would include tuition, books, room and board, and maybe even wages that could have been earned during the time spent in school. Adjusted for inflation, the sum would be either impressive or depressing depending on your point of view. But, I could not begin to put a dollar figure on the value of that education. I met my wife at college and made other life-long friends. We decided to make ministry our life, and we learned how to learn. I even learned something of how much I don't know and may never learn. Those things I have filed in my mind under "PRICELESS."

Impact

For everyone to whom much is given, from him much will be required; and to whom much has been committed, of him they will ask the more.

Luke 12:48

There are many ways to phrase the great question of personal meaning. Do I matter? What do I do that matters? If I left this world today, would it matter? What have I ever done that matters? Feel free to add to the following list.

We are tempted to believe we don't matter. If we don't matter, then why try? If we don't matter, then why care? If we don't matter, whatever we do or fail to do won't change anything anyway. Even if we treat life like a Greek tragedy and dutifully fulfill our respective roles, the ending is still the same. If we rebel to the fullest, that doesn't change things either.

One of God's greatest gifts to us is the assurance that we matter to Him. It begins in the Bible's first chapter: "So God created man in His own image; in the image of God He created Him; male and female He created them" (Gen 1:26–27). This could have been said more succinctly, but brevity wasn't God's goal here. There's purposeful repetition for emphasis. God doesn't want us to miss the point of our unique connection to Him.

Psalm 8 continues the theme. Verse four poses the question, "What is man that You are mindful of him, and the son of man that You visit him?" The answers are amazing:

- "For You have made him a little lower than the angels" (v. 5).

- "And You have crowned him with glory and honor" (v. 5).

- "You have made him to have dominion over the works of your hands" (v. 6).

God has equipped and enabled us. He has charged us with notable responsibility. We can't read Psalm 8 without thinking of Luke 12:48, "For everyone to whom much is given, from him much will be required, and to whom much has been committed, of him they will ask the more."

From a New Testament perspective, John 3:16, Romans 5:6–11, and Ephesians 2:1–10 reinforce the key concept. We are loved by God, saved by God, and given new life by God. "For we are His workmanship, created in Christ Jesus for good works, which God prepared beforehand that we should walk in them." God has redeemed and re-created us for impact, to make a difference in His world.

The devil may claim that we and our actions don't matter, but God exposes his lie. We find joy in serving God, in making a difference to His glory. Examples abound. Can there be greater impact than helping save a soul (Jam 5:19–20)? Who can weigh the impact of helping a child know God (Eph 6:4)? Jesus lauds the impact of any service in His name (Matt 10:40–42; 25:34–40). Think of Dorcas and the impact of her "ordinary" service (Acts 9:36–43). Only God knows the full and eternal impact of what He helps us do in His name.

Super Dud

Not that I speak in regard to need, for I have learned in whatever state I am, to be content.

Philippians 4:11

After two weeks of extreme hype, the 2014 Super Bowl stood little chance of living up to its billing. Still, I didn't anticipate a super dud of a game. My team lost, but it was worse than that. They were non-competitive and stunningly disappointing.

In this sin-damaged world, life has a way of failing to live up to the hype. The wedding ceremony will be magical with our groom, a gallant knight, and the bride, a princess. But the armor seems to rust, and the glass slipper doesn't fit. Baby comes, the most beautiful baby in the world. But baby is expensive, exhausting, and high maintenance. Our work isn't always appreciated at the level that rewards us. We take a vacation, the flight is delayed, and everyone on the cruise ship gets sick. We go to a movie; it's not nearly as good as the trailer, and cell phones keep ringing.

How do we cope with the stress and strain of such realities? The following suggestions might help:

- *Concentrate less on what we hope to feel.* Concentrate more on the ways we can bring joy to those around us, especially those we love (Phil 2:3–4).

- *Learn to laugh at the absurd.* Sometimes God changes our plans, and it works to great blessing (Acts 16:6–10). Sometimes, we don't have a clue who changed our plans, but we're still wise to wait for God's blessing.

- *Choose to find more joy in God's day-to-day surprises (Psa 19:1).* A multi-colored sunset, heavy on the red. A bluebird on an extra-cold day. Banana pudding at potluck.

- *Remember that it's not about you (me).* There's peace and safety in not always being the center of attention.

- *Find people who are having fun and hope their attitude is infectious.* Some people have a knack for getting life right. God can use them to help the rest of us.

- *Choose to lower your expectations.* Only God is always right. Humans often fall short, even when we try really hard. And we don't always try really hard.

- *Take an adventuring approach.* It works like this—I don't have a clue what to expect today, but God is good. If I walk His way and seek His glory, He will open some unexpected door or provide some unforeseen opportunity.

- *Don't be the cause of the dud, and even if you aren't, don't make it worse.* The super dud Super Bowl led us to wash the dishes and head to bed a bit earlier. We knew we'd read about the game and see the noteworthy commercials again the next day. Final score didn't matter. And there's always next year—if the Lord allows.

- *Remember that much of what we think to be important in the moment doesn't amount to a hill of beans.* Loving God, loving others, and helping people toward heaven are our greater joys. Any day in which we have honored God has been a good day (Matt 5:13–16).

- *What seems to be defeat can end up being a stunning victory.* What others intend as wrong can be reversed by God (Gen 50:19–20).

Peace in Bad Times

Though He slay me, yet will I trust Him.

Job 13:15

Studying the book of Job is both a challenging and a rewarding endeavor. Job's world came apart in cascading catastrophes. His possessions, his children, and his health were gone. His wife urged him to curse God and die. His friends utterly misread the situation and tried to pound Job into admitting that he had broken faith with God. But Job knew that he had not.

Job amazes me. When everything goes bad and feels bad, Job still believes that God was good. Though Job pushes the envelope in insisting that God give him an explanation for his pain, Job never stops believing. He never stops believing that God is, that God is good, that God is powerful, and that God can save.

While we know parts of the reason for Job's loss from chapters 1 and 2, to the best of our knowledge Job never knows those answers. He labors under the assumption that knowing the cause of his loss might bring some degree of peace. It's a noble and errant assumption that still tempts us today.

Job's friends amaze me. They are so certain in their conviction that tragedies do not befall the faithful. If catastrophe comes, the victim's personal sin has caused it. Even if humans can't identify the sin, it's stunningly clear to God. If personal sin is the cause, personal repentance is the cure. All Job needs to do to stop his pain is to come clean with God.

In a sense, sin is the cause of all loss. We'll never grasp all the effects of sin on this world. But we know that personal sin isn't the cause of all pain. Jesus never sinned, but endured persecution and a horrible death. Paul wasn't stoned and beaten for his personal sin; rather, he was attacked because of his tireless preaching of the gospel. The innocent infants in Bethlehem didn't die because of evil they had done.

What are we supposed to do with the book of Job? There has to be more than this list, but at least it's a start:

- We remember from chapters 1 and 2 that there's more going on than we can see, hear, or grasp. There's a heavenly realm that's not yet in our view.

- We remember that friends can mean well, try hard, and be dead wrong. Only God is always right.

- We remember that sometimes bad things, terrible things, happen to good people primarily because they are good. Satan loves to harm, and he will do his worst.

- We remember that Satan can't snatch faith from our hearts. Faith can be held and treasured through the darkest of trials.

- We remember to be sure of God, but not overly sure of ourselves. Like Job's friends, we can be sincere, passionate, persistent, and wrong. May God keep us from such harm!

- We remember that we don't always get the answers that we want. We may never know the "why" behind huge events in our lives. Peace comes from being content to let God be God.

No Big Deal?

And whoever gives one of these little ones only a cup of cold water in the name of a disciple, assuredly, I say to you, he shall by no means lose his reward.

Matthew 10:42

Our advancement team came up with a plan to appreciate HCU alumni during "Minister Appreciation Month." Each alumnus for whom we had an address was mailed a lapel pin. When I learned of the plan, my reaction was a vanilla "that's nice"—nothing more.

Turns out that the idea was WAY better than I realized. We've been thanked verbally, by text, by email, and by hand-written note. Kind souls who received the pins have sent generous donations to the university. And I never saw it coming.

I should have known better for a bunch of reasons:

- Good people express appreciation, even for the smallest of gifts. It fits 1 Thessalonians 5:18 and Matthew 7:12.

- No gift given with love, respect, or a pure heart can be small. Think of the boy whose lunch Jesus multiplied to feed thousands. Think of a precious child bringing his mom a dandelion flower or a rock from a nearby stream.

- Genuine expressions of appreciation, especially those that come with no strings or expectations, are rare in this selfish world. Such acts shine in their uniqueness.

- Most people love good surprises, even if some pretend otherwise.

- No gift given to the glory of God or in support of the kingdom can be small. Remember the cup of water

(Matt 10:42) and the widow's small coins (Mark 12:41–44).

- We all like to be remembered. We love to know that people appreciate us. I won't deny that many of my favorite birthday cards come with checks inside, but a check is never owed or expected. In such cases, neither the size of the card nor the amount of the check matters; it really is the thought that counts.

- God uses acts of giving to shape us, bless us, and protect us (Acts 20:35).

- This particular gift was rightly interpreted as affirming, "You belong. You're family."

I got a pin just for being present; though I'm not an alumnus, I work with HCU. An opportunity presented, and I gave it away. It was immediately replaced five-fold. That takes our minds to Luke 6:38, where we're reminded that God has always been the greatest giver.

One of the devil's lies about giving is "go big or go home." He wants us to second guess both our motives and the hearts of those to whom we might give. A little second guessing carries terrible negative weight. It can prevent important actions and quash opportunities for joy.

I'm trying to learn better. If an opportunity to give arises, seize it and enjoy it. Give it to God and let Him do His blessed work. Then, prepare to be impressed.

A Flu Shot and Thanksgiving

In everything give thanks, for this is the will of God in Christ Jesus for you.

1 Thessalonians 5:18

Because I'm on Laura's health insurance, I got my flu vaccine at her school. I never expected to be so entertained. Right after the injection, the nurse told me, "It won't take full effect for two weeks, so avoid exposure until then." The following points are part of what I didn't say to her:

- Yes, I have microscopic vision and can see the flu virus from long range so I can avoid it.

- I have special medical intuition that warns me to avoid people who have the flu.

- Rats, I was planning to visit flu-infested rooms today.

- Does this mean I have a doctor's excuse to hide at home for the next two weeks?

- Where is my virus-rejecting bubble suit?

- Yo, lady. I'm sitting in a middle school library right now. Like there are no germs here?

- So, after the two weeks pass, will it be smart for me to begin visiting flu-infested places?

I try not to say too much to people who play with needles. Bless her heart, the nurse will never know how much she amused me. Not only was I amused, the encounter had other blessings as well. Last year, despite my early arrival, there was a major wait time for the shot. This year, I arrived early and was finished within ten minutes of my appointment time.

Because the nurse told me that the injection might make me feel bad, I received a three-day excuse for being slow with my work and my thinking. She wouldn't put it in print, but that didn't keep me from using it.

Because of the insurance plan, the shot was free. Free is always my favorite price. If the vaccine is effective this year, I'm protected. If it's not, I'm blessed in another way. When I get the flu, I won't feel guilty. I'll be able to tell myself, "You took the shot. You tried. You did your part."

In most situations, there's humor to be found. It seems healthy to find it. In every situation, there are blessings to be found. It's always healthy to see them. In every situation, at least on some level, there are reasons to be thankful. If nothing else, we can be thankful that things aren't worse or that the challenges didn't come earlier. There's great wisdom in choosing to be grateful that things are as well as they are. We can be thankful that we never face trouble alone (Heb 13:5–6). We stay thankful that God's ultimate deliverance is just as certain as His grace, mercy, and love (2 Cor 4:17–5:8; 2 Tim 4:6–8).

Happy Accidents

Every good gift and every perfect gift is from above, and comes down from the Father of lights, with whom there is no variation or shadow of turning.

James 1:17

Some call them happy accidents, but they happen too often to be accidental. Sometimes the quality of blessing is too great to be attributed to mere chance. In the spirit of James 1:17, they turn our minds toward God and hearts toward major gratitude.

We went to Sam's Club just before Christmas a few years back to pick up a few last-minute items. Laura found one of our long-time friends who now lives out of town. What a pleasant encounter, catching up on news, and just being happy to see one another.

I made my annual odd Christmas list of disconnected items. On the list was a boar tusk. I don't think that contributes to poaching or invites animal cruelty. I can remember on the farm back in the day that tusks were periodically cut to prevent major damage to both humans and other pigs. I was a bit surprised when I got an outstandingly ugly boar mask as one of my Christmas gifts. I think the print in my email was too small. The tusk can always come later.

We ate out just after Christmas at one of the usual places—lunch is cheap there. As I looked across the room, we saw two sets of friends whom we seldom find anymore. Laura had a most pleasant visit with them while I "guarded" our table. As we got ready to leave, the server said, "One of our very special customers has taken care of your meal." It's the second time that's happened lately. Nothing accidental about it—people made an obvious choice to be kind—but it sure was a pleasant set of surprises.

Such pleasant surprises aren't limited to things that people do. Remember the last stunning sunset or vibrant rainbow that you saw? Maybe it was a doe and her fawn standing against the tree line. Once for us, it was finding a huge carved water buffalo in a local antique shop. He was just like some we saw outside Cape Town that were way too big to bring home. Same deal with finding a cast iron model of an ancient John Deere tractor at a price we could afford. It obviously belonged in my brother Randy's model tractor collection (Acts 20:35).

I want to cultivate the following attitudes and practices toward life's happy accidents:

- Stay awake for the next blessing. We never know when or where it will come.

- When the blessing comes, savor the moment. Each of those moments is unique and unrepeatable (Eccl 3:1–15).

- When the blessing comes, pause to thank God. He does more to help, bless, and encourage us than we'll ever realize (1 Thes 5:16–18).

- Stay awake for opportunities to bless others. Is there an item, a photo, or a story that should be captured and shared with someone we love (Gal 6:10)?

- Remember that random acts of kindness form just a single category. Calculated acts of kindness can be just as sweet (Heb 10:24).

- Remember that even less-than-happy accidents can come with silver linings. We've all experienced being rescued from ourselves or our circumstances. Once rescued, we're blessed to pay it forward as many times as we can.

On Honesty and Humor

All the days of the afflicted are evil, but he who is of a merry heart has a continual feast.

Prov 15:15

The kid behind the counter asks me, "Would you like fries with that?" He's doing his job. He has no clue that he's presenting an ethical dilemma.

True answer is, "Yes, I'd like fries with that." But it's more complicated than it appears.

- Yes, I'd like fries with that, but my waistline wouldn't.

- Yes, I'd like fries with that, but I'm supposed to be decreasing my triglycerides.

- Yes, I'd like fries with that, but I'm saving the carbs and calories for the candy bar that I'll eat at home.

- Yes, I'd like fries with that, but do you know how much time I'd have to spend on the elliptical to work off that much fat?

I don't want to burden the kid with TMI, but I don't need to harm myself by failing to let what I've learned improve my behavior.

Recently I bought some "way cheap" used books, slightly more than a box full. The cost was $30.05. I handed the clerk $31. She handed me back $.95 and my original $31. I stood there, waiting for her to realize the error. She sat there waiting for me to leave. I finally had to say, "I don't think you meant to give me all this." I think we parted as friends, but sometimes it's hard to tell. We seldom enjoy our own mistakes.

Even more recently, I bought a book for the Overton Memorial Library entitled *The Top Ten Things Dead People Want to Tell You*. The title alone was worth the 50 cents. I love titles that make me think. How could one presume to know the top ten things dead people would want to say? How would one go about polling the dead? If you could, would you poll all the dead since Abel? Would you poll only the righteous dead? How would you guard against multiple responses from the same dead person?

As much as I love the question, why would I think that the dead who don't know me would want to tell me anything? Samuel was not happy when he was disturbed after death (1 Sam 28:15), and we remember that he offered Saul only words of doom. The selfish rich dead man from Luke 16 had a vital message, but he cared only that his five brothers hear it.

Though I haven't yet read the book, I have ideas about what the righteous dead should want to tell us. Think on these ten and add to them.

- Heaven is worth every cost, every condition, and every sacrifice.

- Heaven is richer and more wonderful than words can tell.

- You can't imagine the joy of meeting Jesus face to face.

- The best people who have ever been are here.

- Wow! Those angels can sing.

- The throne of God is way beyond spectacular.

- The new body we're given by God is more than amazing.

- There's nothing bad here: no tears, no pain, no temptation, and no struggles.

- You never have to leave, and you'll never want to leave.

- It really is the home of the soul.

"Criminel" Offenses

Therefore, putting away lying, "Let each one of you speak truth with his neighbor," for we are members of one another.

Ephesians 4:25

S ome phishing emails are easier to spot. A recent one wanted me to send money to avoid "criminel" charges and court costs. Though I don't spell well, I knew something wasn't right.

There's something to say about dumb (should I be kind and say "inattentive"?) criminals. They'll find fewer victims and do less harm. Maybe they'll fail to prosper and choose some honest line of work. Perhaps I'm hoping for too much.

We all know the rule: Cheaters gonna cheat. Liars gonna lie. Takers gonna take. Sometimes their efforts prove clumsy or transparent, and we escape unharmed. Sometimes, they prove smarter than we are, and we "purchase" some expensive education from them.

Of course, the cheaters, liars, and takers fail to account for God, truth, and judgment. Even if they succeed financially, they lose in light of Matthew 16:26 and Revelation 21:8. They miss the blessings of Acts 20:35 and Luke 6:38. Ultimately, they cheat themselves. God is never fooled.

I love straight up, honest people. If you drop your wallet, they hand it back to you with all the cash intact. If you give them too much change, they return the overage. If you agree on a price or a promise, their word is good as gold. "They'll do you any way but wrong" is a favorite description of such good souls.

I was blessed to be reared by straight up, honest people. Is there any way to measure the value of that blessing? How much trouble has it prevented? Would I have chosen honesty and decency had those virtues not been modeled before me from my earliest days? Would I have known the truth of Numbers 32:23 if

I had not been held accountable as a child? What an advantage to learn about life from good and godly parents!

I was also blessed to be reared by believing and balanced parents. They knew about the cheaters, liars, and takers of this world, but they also know the folly of hanging those labels on everyone. From our youth, we heard good people praised for their goodness. Biblical virtues were admired and appreciated. It was the downhome version of "see the virtuous person, be the virtuous person." Aristotle would have been pleased—Jesus too.

I was blessed to be reared by realistic parents. They knew evil existed, and they wanted us to know—not by experience, but in order to avoid pointless pain. They understood 1 Corinthians 15:33. They believed Proverbs 1:10-19, and they taught us to believe as well.

"Treat people right" is a time-honored shorthand version of Matthew 22:39. It's a solid biblical principle that tends to make for peace and good relations. Whenever it seems easier to do otherwise, we need to check our thinking and look for the hook. The cost will exceed the value.

Is it possible that the heart of morality could be this simple? Remember the words of Psalm 15. Psalm 24 is stunningly similar. We honor God when we treat others well (1 John 4:7–11, 20–21). As we show respect and love for those made in the image of God, we show respect and love for God Himself.

Just Odd

For we all stumble in many things. If anyone does not stumble in word, he is a perfect man, able also to bridle the whole body.

James 3:2

Why is it "fiery" and not firey? After all, the root word is fire. Why do we love redundancy so much? Déjà vu all over again. Revert back. Read the following text below. Past history. And don't get me started on future plans. Planning the past seldom works.

Why do we love phrases that are just plain dumb? Football announcers frequently say "young freshman" as if that were outside the norm. The only time it's worth mentioning is when the freshman isn't young. Same deal when they speak of some professional sports star as a "gifted athlete." Non-gifted athletes don't get to be professional sports stars.

Why do some speakers spend precious seconds telling us how little time they have been allotted to speak and how much more they could share if they had more time? Just get on with it.

Any logo or tagline that needs an explanation didn't work. Same with any joke or illustration.

Did you hear about the family who bought a dog at Pet Smart, but it wasn't?

Why is it always way too late when they finally say to us, "To make a long story short"?

Maybe you saw the article about the anti-abortion congressman who resigned after getting caught demanding that his mistress have an abortion. You can't make this stuff up; and if you did, no one would believe you.

When people say to me, "You're looking good," I feel that I've encountered a multiple-choice test. Is it ...

- Exceedingly gracious so that "Thank you" is the proper response?

- Hyperbole mixed with satire?

- A sign of cognitive decline?

- Severely failing eyesight?

- An excellent example of ellipsis? What they really mean is either "You're looking good for a person of your advanced years" or "You're looking good in that I thought you died a few years ago."

I like living on a dead-end street; I either start or end every day by repenting. I like living adjacent to a cemetery; very quiet neighbors, at least so far.

The older I get, the more I'm okay with people asking me for advice and then rejecting it. I don't take it personally, and it leaves me feeling no responsibility for the outcome of their decision.

All this and more is filed under Romans 12:3: "For I say ... to everyone who is among you, not to think of himself more highly than he ought to think...." James 1:19 and 3:2 also fit. None of us is immune.

Balance and Good Judgment

If any of you lacks wisdom, let him ask of God, who gives to all liberally and without reproach, and it will be given to him.

James 1:5

Realism can be both funny and no fun. The early bird gets the worm, but the second mouse gets the cheese. Better thirty minutes early than five minutes late, provided we belong there at all. Here are some other examples of realism:

- If I had done what I "couldda" when I "shouldda," I'd be a happy man right now.

- The operation was a success, but the patient died.

- You will still get a bill in the mail.

- What I should have said right then came to me at midnight, about three days too late.

- What I hoped was my last nerve wasn't.

- Things can almost always get worse—or better.

- I can hear what you want to say loud and clear. Can I find the courage to listen?

- Yes, the Lord delivered him. It was like he fell out of a well.

- A fellow asked a farmer, "What would you do if you had a million dollars?" The farmer's reply: "I guess I'd keep farming until it was all gone."

I'm impressed with "the sons of Issachar who had understanding of the times, to know what Israel ought to do" (1 Chr 12:32). Some are gifted with such insight. I wish I were better at identifying such people. I wish I were better about heeding the counsel of such people. Some just think they understand the times; their confidence is impressive. So is their amnesia. They never seem to acknowledge their errors, and they depend on our accompanying amnesia.

Sometimes the times are easy to understand, but that doesn't mean that we do. Matthew 16:1–4 is stunning. Jesus chided the critical Pharisees: "Hypocrites! You know how to discern the face of the sky, but you cannot discern the signs of the times." They could look skyward and do their own weather predictions, but they ignored God's warnings and instruction. They ignored God's signs while demanding that God give them a sign. Stunningly ironic and stunningly sad!

God's word tells us what we need to know. As needed, God pulls back the curtain to show us His heart and the blessings of trusting Him. But He certainly doesn't tell us everything that we think we want to know. We love Jesus's response to the apostles' question in Acts 1:7: "It is not for you to know the times or seasons which the Father has put in His own authority." Trust Him.

Given God's track record, we know we need to believe what He says. We need to "walk by faith, not by sight" (2 Cor 5:7). We need to welcome God's counsel and guidance (Prov 3:5–8). We need to practice prayerful, humble, and biblically-informed decision making.

Given God's track record and our own, we need to respect God's judgment and realize our limitations. When He chooses to withhold information, that's never capricious or insulting. It's God acting for our good and reminding us of our limits. Perhaps God would give us more insight if we did a better job of respecting what He has said. It's certainly worth a try.

Context and Perspective

Folly is joy to him who is destitute of discernment, but a man of understanding walks uprightly.

Proverbs 15:21

Those who know me well would never offer me a chicken dinner. If avoidable without offense, I don't eat chicken. Same with tofu, beets, onions, liver, celery, and buttermilk. If friends offer me any of those, I assume they're making a joke. If the offer proves serious, then we need to talk.

In a recent meeting, I mentioned that a friend had brought me a bag of turnip greens. From my perspective that is excellent. I'm thinking cornbread and pepper sauce. Perspectives vary. Several in the room confessed that bringing them greens wouldn't be seen as positive at all.

Many people love horses, and they're okay by me. In south Alabama, the standing joke/truism says that the main reason cattlemen lock their pasture gates is that if they don't, someone will leave them a horse.

Upon hearing that I'm from Alabama, people in other states commonly respond with "Roll Tide." I mean no offense, but I left the crimson family decades ago. Laura has a degree from UA, but we met and married in Auburn.

We value context and perspective in many settings. Think of the following:

- Following Paul's inspired teaching in 1 Corinthians 9:19–23, we notice and value context and perspective in evangelism. Within godly limits, we tailor our dress, diet, greetings, and language to fit the sub-culture where we're teaching. Our friends who have recently returned from Haiti, Myanmar, and the Philippines could bear witness to this fact.

- We employ kind judgment in executing Hebrews 10:24: "Let us consider one another in order to stir love and good works." No offense, but it's impossible to encourage me by including me on a fishing trip. I'd be green, and we'd both be miserable. Hebrews 10:24 carries the practical implication that we should know one another well enough to know what encourages vs. discourages. Another example: Some benefit from a public thank you for work well done. Others will work their hearts out, so long as the appreciation is expressed privately.

- We're blessed to make similar application of Ephesians 4:29: "Let no corrupt communication proceed out of your mouth, but what is good for necessary edification, that it may impart grace to the hearers." I'm fine with you saying, "How's it going, BIG GUY?" so long as I don't think you're calling me out on my poundage. Given my poor balance and general clumsiness, it's probably better to avoid, "Looking smooth there, Grace." Sometimes knowing what NOT to say shows great kindness and wisdom.

- Of course we can't omit Colossians 4:6: "Let your speech always be with grace, seasoned with salt, that you may know how you ought to answer each one." Prior communication and level of relationship can help us gauge context and perspective as we follow these fine words. Prayer and knowledge of scripture will certainly help as well. It's a joy to watch wise brethren employ these tools to the glory and honor of Christ. Discerning context and perspective is an art worth learning.

Windy Irony

For we all stumble in many things. If anyone does not stumble in word, he is a perfect man, able also to bridle the whole body.

James 3:2

It happened again with Hurricane Matthew. Reporters travelled into the path of the storm and offered their windblown reports. As usual, the central message was, "Evacuate. Don't put your lives at risk. If you have not evacuated, stay indoors to be as safe as is possible." And by their actions they contradicted their message. They did the very opposite of what they said.

I can't know the motives of each reporter. Perhaps some think they are performing a public service. Perhaps some are just following orders. Perhaps some love the rush of being on the edge of the storm. Some may think themselves immune from harm.

In such cases, I always wonder whether these reporters grasp the irony they portray. I imagine viewers wondering, "Can it really be as bad as they say if they are standing outdoors on live TV telling us about it?"

I admit that I imagine a *Saturday Night Live* skit with weather reporters on the edge of a storm. A sheet of metal roofing severs an arm, so we cut away to our next reporter. A shark glides in on a massive wave and devours him. A swordfish spears a third correspondent. And the guy back in the studio says, "We'll be right back after this brief commercial break. Don't go away." I'm not wishing them harm, but they are indeed tempting fate.

I see similar irony at hospitals. We observe patients outside, smoking—with their IV-poles in tow. On another front, one of the reasons I avoid all-you-can-eat buffets is to prevent my participation in over-the-top irony. Similarly, I resist supersizing the fries with my burger and diet cola.

Christians are in no way immune from stunningly ridiculous irony:

- We sometimes angrily yell at our children, "YOU KNOW I LOVE YOU!!!"

- We sometimes fail to pray even though we actually believe that Luke 18:1, 1 Thessalonians 5:18–19, and 1 Timothy 2:1–4 are teachings inspired of God.

- We sometimes sing, "Give Me the Bible," but fail to open it except during worship.

- We sometimes sing, "All to Jesus I Surrender" and "He Is My Everything," but act like Luke 12:15 and 1 Timothy 6:6–10 aren't accurate.

- We sometimes criticize "what they are doing down at the church," when we know that we—all saved people (Acts 2:47)—constitute the church.

- We sometimes express our economic dissatisfaction (we complain and "poor mouth") when we know that we are stunningly blessed both here (Matt 6:30–34; 1 Tim 6:8) and in the world to come (Matt 6:19–21).

We never want to participate in irony that causes people to doubt the power and veracity of God's word. We never want to be the source of or the excuse for confusion and unbelief.

Thrifty

Give, and it will be given to you: good measure, pressed down, shaken together, and running over will be put into your bosom. For with the same measure that you use, it will be measured back to you.

Luke 6:38

I think of myself as thrifty, but I'm not offended if others think of me as cheap. Bargains are cool. "Why pay retail?" still makes good sense to me.

Recent thrift store shopping has been particularly pleasant. We found a brown cow with excellent horns. That stuffed animal will go to one of the nieces on the farm. I found three Tiggers for Laura. I'm an Eeyore, but Laura likes Tiggers too. We got several books that have been added to the Heritage Marriage and Family Resource Center within the Overton Memorial Library. Laura bought a mink collar on one of the hottest days of June. We love irony.

Every now and then someone hears about my choice to give away something I've purchased at a thrift store and asks, "Aren't you afraid that the recipient of a gift from a thrift store might be insulted?" Not really, for a bunch of reasons:

- Basic honesty. We'd never pretend that a second-hand item wasn't second-hand (Eph 4:25).

- Limited scope. For any important occasion, Laura wouldn't let me buy a second-hand gift. She tries hard to protect me from myself. Sometimes she succeeds (Prov 31:10–12).

- Basic fairness. I buy stuff for myself at thrift stores. I don't mean any insult when I do the same for others (Matt 7:12).

- The surprise factor. Most people like being thought about. They don't look at the origin or cost of the gift.

They are kind enough to be happy to be remembered (Phil 2:13–14).

- No strings. If you like any gift that I give you, cool. If you don't and want to re-gift, donate, or discard it, fine with me. I enjoyed the giving. It's up to you to enjoy the receiving (Acts 20:35).

- No guilt. When I buy something intending to give it away, I feel good. Nothing that's intended to bless, confuse, or amuse a friend involves wasted funds. The smile alone is worth the cost. Some of the puzzled looks are priceless (Heb 13:16).

- Treasure hunting. Every now and then, we find something that qualifies as a treasure. Admittedly, it's a small treasure, but it's still a blessing. My M&M tie remains among the best purchases ever. The big carved water buffalo will always be special.

- Serendipity. On one of our last thrift outings, we found friends in each of the three stores we visited. These were pleasant people we're always happy to see. Laura got to speak highly of one of her students in front of his mom. We love these sweet unplanned and unplannable moments. They remind us of how good God is to us in all things, both big and small (Mal 3:10).

How Are You?

*Beloved, I pray that you may prosper in all things and be in
health, just as your soul prospers.*

3 John 2

Being odd, I tend to enjoy being asked, "How are you?" Actually I appreciate being asked, and I enjoy searching for new ways to respond. Here are some of my favorites:

- "Better than I deserve." Hardly original, but always accurate.

- "Fair to middlin'." Again, not original, but highly functional. It's seriously southern and open to the broadest of interpretations.

- "Peaceable." Enough people have heard me say this, that they're no longer surprised by it. I like it in light of the blessing of Matthew 5:9 and the commandment of Romans 12:18. Since Jesus is "The Prince of Peace," His disciples should be fundamentally peaceable.

- "Better than yesterday." Applicable only when true, and subject to the natural response of, "So how bad was yesterday?" Sometimes that question is welcome, and sometimes I need to let the past be the past.

- "Not as good as I'm gonna be." This one is fun because of its optimism. It's powerful when paired with the stunningly rich promises of 1 John 3:1–3 or 1 Corinthians 15:50–58.

- "Fat and happy." Too often that's literally true, but there are many ways to be "fat."

- "Confused." I really like "dazed and confused," but the combination is less frequent. The confused part applies to some part of almost every day.

- "Blessed." Aren't we all (Matt 5:45)? And aren't all Christians stunningly blessed (Eph 1:3–12; 2:8–10)?

- "Busy and glad to be." I don't just mean engaged in the rat race. I'm thinking more in terms of Luke 2:49 and John 9:4.

- "I'm just proud to be here." Minnie Pearl had it right. There's wisdom in being grateful to still be around and aware.

- "Strange and stranger." I mean this to affirm individual uniqueness. If I offer this answer, I can't rightly take offense if those who hear it agree.

- "If I were any better, I'd have to be twins." I never use this one, but I often hear it.

- "Still learning." I hope this one is true for each of us for all our lives, not in the sense of 2 Timothy 3:7, but definitely in the sense of 2 Peter 1:5–11.

Less than Convenient

I know that whatever God does, it shall be forever. Nothing can be added to it, and nothing taken from it. God does it, that men should fear before Him. That which is has already been, and what is to be has already been; and God requires an account of what is past.

Ecclesiastes 3:14–15

Less-than-convenient stuff happens all the time. There were water meter inspections in our neighborhood, followed by bright blue paint on the curb marking meter locations. We initially missed the fact that new meters were installed.

We knew something was wrong when we heard a strange sound near the washing machine. It wasn't the machine, and there was no water leak in the house. I'm way too old and inflexible for the trip under the house to check the pipes. Besides, the dust under there does crazy things to my breathing.

Found the leak. We know that air got into the lines during the installation of the new meter. Our theory is that the air caused vibration, which caused a weak spot to give way. As we tried to turn our water off, we discovered that the valve at the curb had no handle. We also discovered that none of the wrenches in the house would fit the spindle. We resorted to vice-grips. By this time, it was dark, and Laura was holding the flashlight for me. As I turned the spindle, water sprayed me in the face like a scene from *The Three Stooges*. With help from a neighbor, we finally got the water off for the evening.

What we paid the plumbers was impressive and worth every penny. Being frugal, we had saved a few little plumbing jobs for the next big occasion. None of them merited its own service call. It's one of those, "While they're here, we may as well have them fix the other malfunctioning things, so we get our money's worth." We have learned that all things plumbing-related are way beyond my talent level. And all this was happening on Laura's birthday. We generally have this kind of timing.

Life is often less than convenient. Cars won't start, locks won't open, and lifetime bulbs burn out. Favorite restaurants close or delete their best dishes. The cheap shirt at the discount store comes in every size but yours. Your dog gets fleas. Laura went for a checkup with one of her doctors only to learn that he was no longer with the practice. The nice lady asked, "You didn't get a call?" We don't know if we got a call or not. The answering machine part of our home phone is very independent. Sometimes it deletes messages for us. Sometimes, it hides them from us.

Most of us have been taught the lemonade principle—if life gives you lemons, make lemonade. We all know that's easier said than done. But here's my effort: the leak didn't wet a thing inside our house. We were slightly inconvenienced for only one day. At least we have a house. We tend to get along and enjoy living together in our house. The plumber still comes when we call. We were able to pay the bill. Sinus meds may get me back to normal (at least as close as I get) soon.

The only thing better than the lemonade principle is the thanksgiving principle found in Colossians 3:17 and 1 Thessalonians 5:16–18.

Bottom line: for most of us, the blessings far outnumber the challenges every single day. Even when they don't, the land of rest, peace, and joy is coming. The inconveniences can help us long for that land. They can help us appreciate the people who help us day by day. They can remind us not to get too comfortable here. They can remind us to be good to the folks around us as we seldom know all the ways that life is ganging up on them. And they remind us not to be the source of inconvenience to others, especially to those we love.

Older Isn't Always Wiser

Wisdom is with aged men, and with length of days, understanding.

Job 12:12

In the book of Job, three characters shine: God, Job, and Elihu. Elihu was the youngest of Job's friends. In many respects, he was also the wisest. From Job 32, there are many things we appreciate about Elihu.

- He was properly angry when Job "justified himself rather than God."

- He was properly angry as he saw that Job's friends "found no answer, and yet had condemned Job."

- He was wise to wait until the proper time to offer his wise and needed words.

- And he clearly stated an important truth: "Great men are not always wise, nor do the aged always understand justice" (Job 32:9).

Depending on one's point of reference, I'm either old or rapidly approaching it. And I'm not always wise.

I have a strong preference for reading God's word from a leather-bound book. I'm still trying to adjust to seeing the Bible read from a cell phone or an iPad. Seeing Scripture read from an electronic device just doesn't feel right to me. But I'm trying to get better. I'm learning to be grateful that God's word is being read and respected, whether it's read from a page or from a screen. What God allows had better be OK with me.

I have a strong preference for hearing pages turn as I preach. That sound reminds me of Acts 17:11. I admit that my first thought when I see someone holding a cell phone during a sermon is, "I fear that this person isn't with us right now." But, recently I was reminded that a worshiper was using her cell phone to share the sermon with a friend who was sick at home. Rather than being distracted or disengaged, she was doing just what Hebrews 10:24 and Philippians 2:4 encourage us to do.

It occurs to me that I'm not just getting old in years; I'm also old in style, thinking, and preference. Like you, I know that's not all bad. But we also know that the devil loves conflict, confusion, and disunity. Just as he would divide Jew and Gentile or slave and free during the earliest days of the church, he would happily divide high tech and low tech, cutting edge from old school in this age. So what am I trying to learn?

- Watch my assumptions. Things aren't always as they appear (John 7:24).

- Things don't have to match my style or preference to be acceptable before God (Prov 21:2).

- Think more and speak less (Prov 10:19–21).

- Listen more and longer before I speak (Prov 18:13; Jam 1:19-20).

- It's OK to think more than I say (Prov 17:27–28; 29:11).

- I'd better be very careful of judging a fellow servant of God (Rom 14:1–13).

Revelation 1:3 doesn't limit its blessing to those who read from a pretty leather-bound book. John penned that passage during the days of parchments and scrolls. Methods, tools, and techniques change, but the truth of God stands constant and secure. What an error it would be to let a preference in style cause mistrust or discouragement.

Watching Our Words

Do you see a man hasty in his words? There is more hope for a fool than for him.

Proverbs 29:20

I read it online in an advertisement for a sports celebrity speaker. The man was described as "a former Heisman Trophy winner." Not so, unless the foundation rescinded his award. Same deal when we see someone described as "a former graduate." Unless they took his degree away, he's still a graduate.

Heard someone say, "My heart literally exploded when I heard that news!" Way not so. If his heart had literally exploded, he wouldn't be saying anything—at least not in this world. Hyperbole can be fun, but inaccuracy isn't.

I recently read about a student whose career goals included teaching at "an Ivory League school." I know "Ivy League" was meant, but the misprint still looked funny.

Listened to a news story a few days ago about tornado recovery. The reporter kept talking about the church being destroyed and rebuilt. Biblically speaking, we know the church building was the item under discussion. Jesus didn't die for buildings, and He doesn't save buildings. Thanks be to God that He saves people!

A person recently called school with a question about his transcript. He spoke with our registrar—the person on campus who knows the most about and has the most responsibility for academic records. When he didn't get the answer he wanted, he asked, "Can I speak to the man in charge?" Facts don't change when you ask a different person. It's a great reminder that we not only need to watch our words—we need to watch our attitudes and assumptions as well.

Important things we know about our words and our attitudes:

- Like it or not, our words flow from our hearts. If our hearts aren't right, our words won't be. If our words aren't true and loving, our hearts aren't right. That's Matthew 12:33–37.

- Like it or not, we all err in speech. Since I err, I better not be cruel to you when you make a mistake. We all will be judged by the standard that we apply to others. That's Matthew 7:2.

- Even though all err in speech, I dare not embrace and excuse my errors. Words have too much power to be unleashed without thought and prayer. That's Proverbs 17:27–28, 18:13, and 21:23.

- "Slips of the tongue" are part of what make us funny and interesting. They give us opportunity to accept correction and to say, "Thank you for caring enough to help me." That's Proverbs 10:12 and 17:9–10.

I have referred to Peter as Paul and to Matthew as Mark. I have called people I know well the wrong names and have tried to rename their spouses and children. I need to know that I need God's help and yours in watching my words.

Assumptions

For they had previously seen Trophimus the Ephesian with him in the city, whom they supposed that Paul had brought into the temple.

Acts 21:29

Because we lack perfect knowledge, assumptions may be unavoidable. We may not be aware that we continually hypothesize based both on what we know at the moment and our experience. We test our hypotheses and improve them as we gain more information.

If Laura is late getting home from school, there are numerous reasonable assumptions. She was held up in traffic, she got "picked off" in an unscheduled meeting, the car wouldn't start, or she remembered one more job that needed to be finished before she left her room. There are infinite unreasonable or highly unlikely assumptions: she is purposefully delaying in order to aggravate me, she has run away to join the circus, or aliens have abducted her. It's not a sign of mental or relational good health for me to choose one of those unreasonable assumptions. It's not a sign of spiritual good health for me to choose an assumption that impugns her judgment or character.

In some cases, errant assumptions can kill you. Remember Romeo and Juliet? How many people are killed each year by "unloaded" guns? Think of 1 Samuel 1 and the foolish Amalekite who assumed that David would be happy to hear that he had killed King Saul. He assumed wrongly and lied his way into execution. Remember Haman's assumption in Esther 6? He assumed the king's question flowed from a desire to honor him. Imagine his disgust when he was ordered to honor Mordecai!

Errant assumptions can kill relationships. A friend misses a lunch appointment with me. I assume it's because he no longer values our friendship, or he got a better offer from a better friend, or I'm just not important to him. The judgmental assumption gives me permission to be angry, to think what I shouldn't think, and to say what I shouldn't say. Poor assumptions give place to the devil. They invite the actions condemned in Ephesians 4:31.

If you've ever been given the benefit of the doubt by friends, you know the power of gracious assumptions. You show up late; they know that's out of character, and they're not mad at all. They spent the "wait time" praying for your health and safety. You miss a deadline; they know that's out of character, and they help you complete the project. They don't blow a fuse and, even if they rightly hold you accountable, they don't seek to punish. You know just the opposite if you've been stung by negative false assumptions.

These things I think I know about assumptions:

- We all make them. We're wise to know when we're making them.

- At least some of our assumptions prove to be wrong.

- I'd rather err on the side of grace and kindness than on the dark side.

- I'm wise to treat you just as I'd want you to treat me (Matt 7:12; Phil 2:3–4).

- God doesn't have to make them. God always knows.

The higher our thoughts and motives, the closer we'll be to the heart of God. There's no need to be damaged by unworthy assumptions.

Disingenuous

And the grace of our Lord was exceedingly abundant, with faith and love which are in Christ Jesus. This is a faithful saying and worthy of all acceptance, that Christ Jesus came into the world to save sinners, of whom I am chief. However, for this reason I obtained mercy, that in me first Jesus Christ might show all longsuffering, as a pattern to those who are going to believe on Him for everlasting life.

1 Timothy 1:14–16

We love truth, honesty, and forthrightness. We find those virtues both refreshing and comforting. We hate lies and deception, especially when we realize that someone is trying to play us.

I hate the auto commercials that basically claim, "Hurry down to buy your new car. At these prices, they'll all be gone soon. Don't miss out." News flash: If the cars were selling that fast, they wouldn't waste money on advertising.

We recently received an invitation to a fundraising dinner for a non-profit organization. The literature included a line like, "Tables are sure to sell out. Reserve yours today." I decided that it might be kind NOT to reserve a table. We didn't want to knock others out of their opportunity to attend.

But you are way ahead of me. Those hosting the event had no way to know if it would sell out. Those who created the advertising were following the common path of "let's make this sound so good that people can't resist attending." I found their effort disingenuous.

I love the pattern described by Paul in 1 Thessalonians 2:1–12. Paul risked life and limb to take the gospel to the first century world. Nothing was more important to him than preaching "Christ and Him crucified." But Paul makes it clear that the gospel of Christ must be presented in the context of truth, love, fairness, and honesty. Note the evidence from the text:

- Paul was forthright about persecution he had suffered previously, 2:1–2. He did not try to hide the cost of discipleship. He did not try to hide the risks of obedience.

- Paul would not use deceit or error to make the message more attractive, 2:3–4. His goal was to please God in every way that he could.

- Paul avoided the temptation to become a people pleaser, 2:4–5. As much as he loved to encourage, he would not cross the line into flattery (untruth, exaggeration, distortion, seeking to manipulate).

- As much as Paul loved the brethren and appreciated being loved by them, he refused to seek glory from men, 2:6. Paul knew how fickle people can be. He knew that the Lord both knows and weighs our hearts.

- As powerful as Paul could be as an apostle, a preacher, and a missionary, he refused to bully either potential converts or brethren, 2:7–8. He chose the path of gentleness, comparing his approach to that of a nursing mother. What love could not do, Paul would not do.

- Paul worked hard and used his example to encourage the brethren to work hard, 2:9. He let his example back up his words. He welcomed scrutiny.

- Paul held himself and his fellow evangelists to the same standard that God sets for all believers, 2:10–12. If you ask people to remember "how devoutly and justly and blamelessly we behaved ourselves," you must know that they will. And you know that they would notice inconsistencies if such existed.

Life's Flow

To everything there is a season, a time for every purpose un-
der heaven: a time to be born and a time to die.

Ecclesiastes 3:1

S ome weeks grab your attention more than others. Recently, we visited two funeral homes and attended two weddings within the span of four days. On the day of one of the wed-dings, our nephew and his wife welcomed the birth of their daughter. Within that same week, friends were bruised in a car crash, another friend had surgery, and yet another received a se-rious medical diagnosis. Life's inevitable and unpredictable flow surely makes us think.

We never know what's around the next corner, and that may be a huge blessing (Jam 4:14). It should move us to humility. It should move us to appreciate our wondrously changeless Creator. It surely helps us avoid worry (Matt 6:34). It should always move us to prayer and to gratitude that things are as well as they are.

Parts of life's flow are both pleasant and beautiful. We wel-come the cooler temperatures and the changing of the leaves. If the Lord sends it, we'll enjoy some lovely snowfall this winter. By the time spring comes, we'll need the newness of the first green-gold leaves (think of Robert Frost's "Nothing Gold Can Stay"). We love precious weddings when God blesses young Christians to create new homes. There's nothing more joyous than a birth, whether the arrival of a new child or the new birth that Jesus em-phasized in John 3. There's even a beauty in physical death when it's remembered in light of John 14, 1 Corinthians 15, and Reve-lation 14:13.

Parts of life's flow are unimaginably difficult. The illnesses, ac-cidents, and disappointments of this sin-damaged world often break our hearts. We see people we love enduring unfair trials. Worse, we sometimes see people we love causing great pain. Even worse, we sometimes find ourselves contributing to the trials and pains of others. All this makes us long for the righteousness, purity, and peace of heaven (Rev 21:1–4).

There are at least three things that we want to do in every circumstance of life's uneven flow:

- We want to trust God even more than we trust ourselves (Heb 6:13–20).

- We want to serve God ahead of serving ourselves (Matt 20:20–28).

- We want to love God even more than we love ourselves (Matt 22:34–40).

In terms of what might happen tomorrow, we don't know. In terms of what ultimately happens to all who are saved by grace through faith, we are certain (2 Tim 4:6–8; Rev 2:10b). One day we will awaken in God's tomorrow, in God's presence. One day we will be reunited with all the faithful of all the ages. One day we will see Him face to face, "And thus we shall always be with the Lord" (1 Thes 4:17b).

Your Best Behavior

For the grace of God that brings salvation has appeared to all men, teaching us that, denying ungodliness and worldly lusts, we should live soberly, righteously, and godly in the present age.

Titus 2:11–12

I was hurrying to get home so we could leave for a preaching appointment in Hazel Green. As I rounded a busy corner, a car pulled out across my lane. It was no problem to stop because even my "hurrying" is slow by modern standards. Turns out the car belonged to two sweet Christians. Glad I didn't yell, blow the horn, or otherwise act out. Be on your best behavior; you never know who's watching.

Later that same evening, we were on the way home from the speaking appointment. We were stopped at a traffic light in Athens. Suddenly, there was a slight bump as the vehicle behind us failed to stop in time. The driver walked up with the perfect questions, "Are you OK? Are you sure?" As we affirmed that we were OK, his next line was, "Bill, is that you?" There was no damage, but we had been tapped by a fellow preacher. Glad we kept our cool. Be on your best behavior; you never know who's watching.

I've learned some interesting things about driving (and other) mistakes:

- We all make them. John 8:7 should keep us on our best behavior.

- I'd rather be the "victim" of a driving mistake than to be the one who made the error. Maybe that's pride or ignorance, but it seems easier to grant forgiveness than to need it. It's always a blessing to be able to extend grace to others (Gal 6:10).

- Stuff is just stuff. "One's life does not consist in the abundance of things that he possesses" (Luke 12:15).

All stuff is going to perish. Stuff is never as important as people.

- Most of us don't multitask well. Most of us are better when we focus on one thing at a time. We need to keep first things first.

- No matter how much I tell myself to "expect the unexpected," the unexpected always surprises me. I'm glad God knows the future, and I'm certain I don't. It's good to know our limitations.

- How we handle unpleasant surprises says a lot to the world around us. If we maintain composure and civility, things go a lot better (Eph 4:26–32). Calm, measured behavior might show others that we know Jesus (Acts 4:13).

- Everything that happens to us offers us an opportunity to learn. We strongly prefer the light and easy lessons, but we often grow more from the challenging ones.

- Many seemingly negative events serve as reminders of God's goodness, God's grace, and God's truth. Anything that brings us closer to God is ultimately a blessing (Phil 1:12–18; 4:12–13).

It's wise to behave and think before speaking (Jam 1:19) because we never know who's watching—a lost soul who needs a reason to believe, a struggling brother who needs a reason to hold on, a family member who needs one more example of Christianity in action. It's wise to behave and think before acting because we know who's always watching. God never misses anything (Psa 139:1–6).

Hard "Road" to Hoe?

Whoever guards his mouth and tongue keeps his soul from troubles.

Proverbs 21:23

It's one of the better education publications that I receive, always helpful and thought-provoking. And the teaser for one recent article mentioned the fact that Benjamin Franklin was correct when he described philanthropy as "a hard road to hoe." It might be a hard road to travel or even a hard road to find, but the saying that the author meant to use is "a hard row to hoe." Back in more labor-intensive days, people hoed the weeds and grass out of rows of their crops. While I suppose it's possible that a road has for some reason at some time been hoed, that would be way too rare an event to become an established figure of speech.

I've been pondering the "hard road" and the "hard row." The confusion is understandable; the two words sound a bit alike. In our daily lives, roads are more common than rows. But there's more to it than that. Consider the following:

- How often do I hear what I expect to hear? One celebrity put it like this: "I am listening, but I only hear what I want to." Critical listening is a great and challenging skill (Luke 8:18).

- How effective am I at self-correction? In so many cases, we don't know what we don't know. There's no reason for us to check what we believe to be correct. We don't even stop to ask, "Why would a road need hoeing? Does this make sense?" (Psa 139:23–24)

- Do I realize how easy it is for me to get things wrong? God's perfection is part of His beauty. It draws us to Him (Psa 50:2).

- What do I do when I find a mistake? More tellingly, what do I do when someone else finds one of my mistakes and brings it to my attention? Correctability is a wonderful asset. No need to defend an error. If it's wrong, it's wrong. No need to question the motives of the one who found the error. It saves time and pain to assume good motives, to express sincere appreciation, and to thank the Lord that we blessed someone by allowing that person to help us (Prov 9:8; 13:18; 15:31–32; 17:10; 27:5).

All of us who write, speak, or teach regularly make mistakes. This book went through multiple reviews and improvements before it reached print. I like the process. It produces a better product. It involves, includes, and values others. It helps protect against pride. And it's a sound application of 1 Peter 5:5–6: "Yes, all of you be submissive to one another and be clothed with humility, for God resists the proud, but gives grace to the humble. Therefore humble yourself under the mighty hand of God, that He may exalt you in due time." Pride is the "hard road."

I Wish

*For this is good and acceptable in the sight of God our Savior,
who desires all men to be saved and to come to the knowledge
of the truth.*

1 Timothy 2:3–4

I wish people were as afraid of sin as they are of Ebola. I don't mean to make light of the deadly virus. We're all wise to pray for the quick discovery of an effective vaccine. We certainly admire the courage of those who care for Ebola victims.

But we know that as bad as it is, Ebola can't touch one's soul. It can't separate a person from God. It can't cause spiritual death. As bad as Ebola is, it can't hold a candle to either the world-wide or the personal effects of sin.

I wish people cared as much about spiritual security as they do about physical and financial security. Matthew 6:19–20 is stunningly clear on the limitations of earthly (physical, finite, material) treasures. Treasures can decay through multiple means. Or thieves can take them. Spiritual treasures are different. Not to sound irreverent, but everything is totally safe in the First Bank of Heaven.

We know the other truth about material treasures. If they don't leave us, we leave them. Neither they nor we are permanent here.

I wish people wouldn't demean others based on racial or ethnic differences. Genesis 1:26–27 applies to every race—each is equally made in the image of God. Acts 17:26 supports that conclusion.

To dehumanize a person based on color, tribe, or national origin is ungodly at its core. Just as the Great Commission passages state, God sends His gospel to "all the nations" (Matt 28:19) and "to every creature" (Mark 16:15). Jesus sends us to "the end of the earth" with His saving message (Acts 1:8).

I wish people would learn the joy of giving. We have God's word on it: "It is more blessed to give than to receive" (Acts 20:35). Selfish taking puts us at the center of a very small and God-less universe. Giving as God ordains opens the very windows of heaven (Mal 4:10; 2 Cor 9:6–15).

I wish people would learn the blessings of peace. Be a peacemaker, and God will acknowledge you as His child (Matt 5:9). Of course, this presupposes that we have chosen to believe and obey Jesus, "the Prince of Peace" (Isa 9:6). It welcomes the promise of John 14:27, "Peace I leave with you, My peace I give to you; not as the world gives do I give to you. Let not your heart be troubled, neither let it be afraid."

I wish people would value the spiritual peace of being reconciled to God (Romans 5:6–11) and the value of pursuing peace with men (Rom 12:9–21).

I wish people would recognize the folly of vengeance. "Getting even" never works. What looks "even" to one side will always seem extreme and unfair to the other. Vengeance, even the desire for vengeance, damages everyone involved. And it communicates a fundamental mistrust and misunderstanding of God (Rom 12:12–21). God won't ever ignore justice, but He "desires all men to be saved and to come to the knowledge of the truth" (1 Tim 2:4).

If God can find it in His heart to forgive those who crucified His Son, we can find it in our hearts to forgive those who wrong us. What we wish for others, we are blessed to make real in our lives.

Clear Communication

For the hearts of this people have grown dull. Their ears are hard of hearing, and their eyes they have closed, lest they should see with their eyes and hear with their ears, lest they should understand with their hearts and turn, so that I should heal them.

Matthew 13:15

From time to time we hear a variation of the semi-famous saying, "I know that what you think you heard is not what I think I meant to say." Communication is complicated. It often doesn't proceed as intended.

On a trip through Tennessee, a friend noticed the following wording on a beauty salon sign: "Brading Hair." We think they meant braiding hair. "Brading" sounds like something you'd do with rivets. Most people wouldn't pay to have that done to their heads.

Decades ago, I passed around a list at a devotional, asking people to sign up to bring deserts to the next meeting. I meant desserts (sweets), not deserts (cacti, sand, lizards). Before the list got back to me, it had drawings (glaring sun and a cactus) and questions (Mojave? Sahara?) pointing out my error.

Back in the day before cell phones and GPS, did you ever try to give or get directions? "Go to the third or fourth red light and kinda turn left, but not real left." Multiple guess is not desirable. What if the light isn't red? (Yes, I know that's a bit too literal, but I have been asked that question.) What's a "kinda turn"?

One of my all-time favorite communication quotes is, "Communication is an art; become an artist." I love the wisdom, but I find it extremely challenging to put into practice. What seems clear and congruent to me often doesn't work so well for others. There's another quote that I believe but don't enjoy: "What can be misunderstood will be misunderstood." I think it's a corollary of Murphy's Law. I know it's a fact.

Mark 16:15–16 seems so clear to me. "Go into all the world and preach the gospel to every creature. He who believes and is baptized will be saved; but he who does not believe will be condemned." I'm amazed at the questions and comments I've heard about this passage:

- Is "go" an accurate translation, or should it be "as you are going"? Might both be proper for us to practice?

- Is "the gospel" just the death, burial, and resurrection of Jesus (1 Cor 15:1–6) or does it include all the "doctrine of Christ"? Of course that draws the follow-up question. Is "the doctrine of Christ" all the biblical teaching about Jesus or does it include all that Jesus had disciples teach in His name?

- If baptism is part of the process of salvation, then why doesn't Mark 16:16 say, "but he who does not believe and is not baptized will not be saved"? Really? Why would someone who does not believe consider being baptized? (Col 2:12; Acts 16:30–35)

How we must try God's patience with our communication shortcomings! We often don't listen well. We let what we want to hear (what we prefer) slant how we listen. We tend to relativize and water down things that make demands on us. We tend to "over-hear" (over-apply, wrongly apply) teachings that agree with what we prefer to believe. We often hear out of context. We often don't hear at all.

Jesus often said, "He who has ears to hear, let him hear." He urged us to be careful how we hear, what we hear, and who we hear (Mark 4:24; Luke 8:18; 10:16). And He also warned us to be careful of our words (Matt 6:33–37; 12:33–37). We need to respect, appreciate, learn from, and heed God's clear communication. And we need to imitate His excellent example in both word and deed.

Real Food

Do not labor for the food which perishes, but for the food which endures to everlasting life, which the Son of Man will give you, because God the Father has set His seal on Him.

John 6:27

The banana pudding at a recent church potluck could make a fellow hurt himself. It was that good—in a class with what my mother makes.

Had some shrimp and grits a few days ago. Too expensive, but too good to pass up. I look forward to going back for more.

On the flip side, the bratwurst looked so good in the package. On top of that, they were a bit cheaper than expected. We should have paid more. They just weren't quite right.

Most of us enjoy good food, but we know the fellowship at potlucks enhances the cuisine. It's the same with all family gatherings. Everything is better when shared with people you love.

As surely as there's food that's good for the body, there's also food that's good for the soul. It's wonderful when Christians embrace the truth of John 4:32–34, when doing God's work is more fulfilling than food, money, or human accomplishment. It's wonderful when Christians realize that the bread of life is more important than life itself, that the bread of life ultimately satisfies forever.

There's also food that's good for the spirit. Some food stirs memories of simpler and happier times. It reminds us of people we'd love to see again, whether in this life or the one to come. It reminds us of people who love us and will always love us. It reminds us of works that we have shared to the glory of God.

Sometimes the food seems odd to us—garri, fufu, and pounded yam (Nigeria), birthday cake with cabbage in the middle (Russia), snoek and chakalaka (South Africa), or stuff that's been rescued from brackish water (Bangladesh). I guess grits, collards, and pickled peaches would seem just as odd to them. Odd or not, we welcome such blessings even when they don't match our taste buds. We welcome them because the people who share them are our family in Christ. Their work is our work because it's God's work.

Pray that God will help us desire the real food, the food that does not perish because it leads to everlasting life. Hungry souls all over the world need that nourishment. And we get to help them find it.

On Waiting

Wait on the Lord; be of good courage, and He shall strengthen your heart; wait, I say, on the Lord!

Psalm 27:14

Knowing that doctors' offices tend to run behind, Laura and I each took books to her latest appointment. The first lady who showed up in our room commended that choice. There's an old adage, "The secret of patience is to do something else in the meanwhile." That may not be the whole truth, but we find that it works quite well.

As Christians, we are blessed with so many good things to do "in the meanwhile." We can pray. We can make our prayer list. We can work on our next Bible class. We can contemplate the goodness of God. We can write cards to people who need our encouragement. We can write the next bulletin article. We can count our blessings. We can relive and re-enjoy some of our blessings. We can memorize a favorite passage. We can plot new ways to "encourage one another to love and good works" (Heb 10:24). We can remember times that God has rescued us. We can contemplate the nobility and selflessness of God's wondrous grace.

As I write this, Laura's upcoming surgery is some thirty days away. When people hear that, they tend to respond kindly: "I'm so sorry that you're having to wait." Laura doesn't view it that way. Her response is in the range of, "No, it's a blessing. There are tons of things that I want to do before July 31." Our attitude while we wait is HUGE.

What are the best actions and attitudes to choose while waiting?

- *What we can't change, we can't change.* In those cases, acceptance is a wonderful virtue. What is, is—whether we like it or not. Acceptance is not agreement. Acceptance is choosing to work within God's reality.

- *Would it be okay if we called prayerfulness an attitude?* Choosing to be quick to pray, choosing to be frequent in prayer, and choosing to pray whenever an opportunity presents can do nothing but bless us.

- *Choosing to value opportunities above obstacles is also most wise.* If we must wait, what can we learn while waiting? Whom can we serve while waiting? How can we grow while waiting? Denying obstacles doesn't work. It's less than honest and it has us focusing on the negative. Staying busy seizing opportunities is far more proactive than focusing on obstacles.

- *Owning our feelings can also bless us.* It sure beats denying or stuffing them. Feelings come and go. They can range from the peaks to the pits. Feelings are just what they are; they are not choices, actions, or sins. Different folks ex press their feelings in radically different ways. So long as those expressions aren't unfaithful to Christ, there is no harm.

- *Listening while we wait can bless us in countless ways.* We will hear some of the sweetest prayers and compliments. We will hear heartfelt truth from surprising sources. Being among Christians, we will hear loads of love. Being among fellow humans, we will also hear some most discouraging "clanks." Some of us choose to count the clanks and to rank them from funniest to worst. We wouldn't recommend that for everyone, but it can be a fine distraction as we seek to turn potential negatives into sources of humor education.

- *We can remember the great waiters within Scripture.* Think of Abraham and Sarah, Zacharias and Elizabeth, Moses, Daniel, and more. Their patient expectation strengthens our hearts.

- *We can review our favorite waiting passages.* Certainly Isaiah 40:31 comes to mind: "But those who wait upon the Lord shall renew their strength." When we have to wait, we're blessed to wait upon, with, and for the Lord.

Learning from the Fridge

Do not judge according to appearance, but judge with righteous judgment.

John 7:24

Aafter twenty-five years of faithful service, our refrigerator died. Its death was not unexpected. The icemaker quit working years ago. The seals were leaky. From time to time it warned us with un-interpretable noise.

An afternoon of shopping led to the choice of a new fridge. But the store didn't have our size and style in stock. "It'll have to be ordered." Delivery was set for the next Friday with the promise, "The delivery guys will call you to set up a convenient time." We provided multiple telephone numbers. And there's the rub.

The delivery guys didn't call the first number listed. Instead, they left a message on the answering machine, "We'll be there on Friday between 10:00 and 2:00." Immediately, I assume that I'll be losing half a day at work. In that I work ten minutes from home, all they had to do was call my cell as they left the warehouse. But there was no way to speak to the delivery guys. All their call back numbers are "fully automated for my convenience." So, what can be learned from the fridge and its friends?

Within any group, any individual has strong ability to make others look good or bad. I give the salesman credit for speaking in good faith. I think he really believed that the delivery guys would talk to us before setting a time. But when they didn't, the whole organization looked bad. Do I remember this truth when it comes to upholding the honor and reputation of church? Of my family? Do I set others up for disappointment (1 Pet 2:13–16)?

People love to talk to people. We don't like talking to machines, even our own machines. The personal touch matters. Do I remember this when visitors grace the assembly? Do I remember to be attentive with greetings, calls, visits, and prayers (Heb 10:24; Phil 2:3–4)?

People hate to be presumed upon. Clearly the delivery guys never thought, "These folks have nothing better to do on Friday than to wait for us to come," but the phone call made it look like that. Do I take people for granted? If so, how do I think they feel? Do I properly consider how my actions look to others (Matt 7:12)?

Turns out the actual delivery guys were not the ones who made the call. They were polite and professional. They came within the first hour of the proposed time. They did a lot to improve my attitude. What effect do I have on others? Do my words and my conduct draw people toward Jesus (Acts 4:13)? Does my conduct make the church look good?

In Praise of Cheating?

You shall not cheat your neighbor, nor rob him.

Leviticus 19:13a

I read the article online back in 2018. If the article is correct, during a Mets-Dodgers baseball game, the Mets' third baseman missed catching a foul ball that was hit into the stands. Rather than acknowledging that, he grabbed a kid's youth-league ball, showed it to the umpire and then tossed it back into the stands. The out was recorded.

Those actions trouble me, but not nearly as much as the wording of the article. The author labeled this deceptive, unsportsman-like act "good, old-fashioned gamesmanship." He continued: "It was easily the best deception of the MLB season."

If the player cheated, we decry his lack of ethics and his lack of respect for the game. Whether cheating happened or not, we decry the author's lack of ethics. He praised dishonesty. He approved dishonesty by labeling it "gamesmanship."

But you know what some people say:

- If you're not cheatin', you're not tryin'.

- It's not cheatin' if you don't get caught.

- All's fair in love and war.

- What right do you have to impose your values on others?

- You have no right to judge.

I beg to differ. We prefer, promote, and practice a radically different set of values:

- Winners never cheat, and cheaters never win. They may win a moment or a game, but ultimately the law of sowing and reaping—what some call karma—proves true.

- Sin (any wrongdoing) is always pre-caught. God knows it happened, and so does the perpetrator.

- When rules and fundamental fairness are disrespected, everybody loses. Such disrespect invites selfishness and abuse. Ultimately, it harms everyone.

- There are fundamental values within the hearts of good people. There are things that we innately know to be wrong.

- It's not wrong to call wrong wrong. It's neither unfair nor unrighteous judgment to uphold fair standards of conduct.

But you know that it would be unfair to stop without asking these questions:

- Does my personal ethical conduct meet the standard of the Golden Rule (Matt 7:12)?

- Do I have one set of rules for myself, but a different set for others (Matt 7:1–5)?

- Do I take proper responsibility for both my actions and my motives (Prov 16:2; 21:2)?

- Is my conduct the same in public (in front of witnesses) as in private (Mark 4:22; 1 Cor 4:5)?

- Do I realize that my actions shape my character and my reputation (Prov 20:11)?

- Do I know that sin, (unfairness, injustice, dishonesty) never pays (Prov 10:2–3; 13:11)?

- Do I think God doesn't know when my actions dishonor Him (2 Cor 5:10)?

Math Matters

Then one poor widow came and threw in two mites, which make a quadrans. So He called His disciples to Himself and said to them, "Assuredly, I say to you that this poor widow has put in more than all those who have given to the treasury."

Mark 12:42–43

A couple of days before Christmas, a strange news story caught my eye. It seems that 3,200 prisoners in the state of Washington were prematurely released because someone miscalculated their sentences under a court ruling which mandated that "good behavior" be factored into sentence length. Stunningly amazing and stunningly human.

The story brings several thoughts to mind:

- Metaphorically speaking, it pays to measure twice and cut once.

- Truthfully speaking, there are three kinds of people in this world: those who can do math and those who can't.

- Speaking from the perspective of Murphy's Law, if it can go wrong, it will.

- Realistically speaking, what's the solution? Is there a solution? Do you make all the released inmates come back to prison?

- Responsibly speaking, if your math skills work, is there a math teacher whom you should send a note of thanks?

- Interpersonally speaking, I won't be insulted if you check my math. I have been wrong before, and I will be wrong again.

- Technologically speaking, I wonder if they'll blame the computer.

- Bureaucratically speaking, I wonder if they'll appoint a commission or a taskforce to investigate this error. I also wonder how much that will cost the taxpayers.

I'm not gloating; neither am I insulting the State of Washington. When it comes to important and embarrassing errors, no one is immune. To quote the great philosopher Clint Eastwood, "A man's got to know his limitations."

As a rule, math is quite logical. Biblically speaking, math doesn't always follow those rules. Maybe that's just as it should be, reminding us of the limits of our logic.

- Sometimes one equals three and three equals one. Think of the Trinity.

- Sometimes two equals one. Think of husband and wife according to Genesis 2:24.

- Sometimes 66 equals one. One Bible, sixty-six books.

- I love the king's math problem in Daniel 3:24–25. Glad he figured it out.

- I don't even know what to say about the math of 2 Peter 3:8 and Psalm 90:4.

Minor Medical Adventures

For You formed my inward parts; you covered me in my mother's womb. I will praise You, for I am fearfully and wonderfully made; marvelous are Your works, and that my soul knows very well.

Psalm 139:13–14

Because of my brother's recent bypasses, my doctor expressed strong interest in having my heart checked. Because this agreed with my parents' wishes, I chose to cooperate. Thus the minor medical adventures began.

Turns out that I don't qualify for a stress test due to lack of symptoms. That doesn't grieve me at all. I had a stress test once, years ago. I found it surprisingly non-stressful. As per usual, my blood pressure was a bit high in the doctor's office. It's generally well-behaved at home, so I've diagnosed myself with "white coat syndrome." You can google it.

Thanks to Laura's good insurance, I did qualify for an echocardiogram and a carotid duplex. It's strange to lie on a table and watch images of your heart function. I found it entertaining that some of the images looked like moving Rorschach cards. It's amazing to learn how much a simple and non-invasive test can reveal.

I also qualified to wear a heart monitor for 48 hours. Getting it required a trip to the main medical office "across from the Cox Boulevard church building." If you pass the church building, go another quarter-mile, skip the building on the boulevard, and find the bigger building behind the medical offices, it is "across from" that church building. I will admit wondering if this was part of the stress test that I didn't qualify for.

I'm glad I'm ambulatory, as the testing part of the medical complex was "take a left, take the second hallway to the right, at the end of that hall go left, sign in, sit down." To do that, you walk through two seas of humanity (obvious exaggeration) in large waiting rooms. My waiting room was far smaller and filled with some really pleasant people.

Half an hour later, the nurse called for "Regents." Turns out that was me. With a last name like Bagents, you learn to be imaginative. Wore the monitor, took the tests, and I seem to be relatively OK for the shape that I'm in. I'm also more grateful than I was.

- To date, I've spent amazingly little time in medical offices. Most of my time with doctors has been waiting with others. Six decades of health is a HUGE blessing.

- When I visit medical offices, they're happy to see me. I have enough plastic in my pocket to keep the financial relationships going.

- So far, I'm able to walk in and walk out. All my medical adventures have been minor.

- I know it won't always be that way. Unless the Lord returns soon or I die suddenly, my health will eventually erode.

I hope my minor medical adventures will give me more compassion and understanding for those whose adventures aren't minor. I hope my minor issues will make me more thankful for my current level of health and strength. I hope my minor adventures will keep reminding me to pray for friends and brethren who face struggles that I can't begin to understand. I hope we all realize and remember that we aren't permanent here. Our forever home with God awaits us (2 Cor 5:1–8; John 14:1–4). That home will be sweeter than our very best dreams.

Making My Head Hurt

Then Samuel went to Saul, and Saul said to him, "Blessed are you of the Lord! I have performed the commandment of the Lord." But Samuel said, "What then is this bleating of the sheep in my ears, and the lowing of the oxen which I hear?"

1 Samuel 15:13–14

A recent email solicitation reminded me that there are 86,400 seconds in a day. It was an offer to help me use each of them more efficiently. I want to be more efficient, but I know I'm not that good. Besides, most days I sleep about 25,000 of those seconds. Time is precious, and it's a gift from God. But humans are not such efficient creatures.

Recovering from foot surgery led to the watching of too many *Gunsmoke* episodes. I like old Westerns, but then I started thinking. Why does much of the action center around the Long Branch Saloon? Was the promotion of drinking and gambling as normal and harmless activities intentional? Why did it take me so long to ask myself this question? Why am I not more awake and thoughtful regarding the subtle messages being promoted in the media? What weird ideas wander in when I'm less than awake? The next time you watch an old movie, notice how everyone smokes and looks cool doing it. Notice how many lies seem justified or necessary.

In a different vein, why was Doc's office upstairs? How does it make sense to carry every sick and injured patient up those steep steps? How many of my habits, choices, and preferences make just as little sense? Whatever I grow accustomed to seems normal to me. It's amazing what we can come to perceive as normal.

Perhaps you saw the interview where the third-party presidential candidate was asked about Aleppo, Syria, arguably the epicenter of the ISIS crisis at the time. He had the blankest look and asked in all honesty, "What is Aleppo?" I've had that blank look—more than once. I've been just as lost in the moment as the candidate was. And I hate such moments. If possible, I'd pay good money to ensure that I never have such a moment again. At the same time, I recognize that those moments have their benefits. They serve to humanize us and to make us remember that we certainly don't know it all. In the moment—in any moment—any of us can "gap out."

I'm not at all fond of professional politicians—major understatement. Many recent gaffes by politicians remind me of how happy I am that my every word isn't digitally-recorded and every phrase parsed without regard to context. James 3 reminds us that no one can stand up to such scrutiny. There are words I wish I had back. There are words I should have said but didn't. There are words that others heard in ways I never intended. And there are words that kind souls chose to hear far better than I knew how to convey. All this makes me appreciate forgiveness and opportunities to try again (Eph 4:29–31; John 13:1–9).

Outlook

*But the Lord said to Samuel, "Do not look at his appearance
or at his physical stature, because I have refused him. For the
Lord does not see as man sees; for man looks at the outward
appearance, but the Lord looks at the heart."*

1 Samuel 16:7

Sometime back, I lost the big toe on my right foot. It wasn't
much fun. The doctor kept calling it "the great toe." Since it
was plaguing me, I couldn't describe it as "great." Vocabulary and perspectives vary.

Soon after, I chose to drive myself to the retina specialist. It
was my first post-surgical drive. They dilated my eyes of course.
As I left the office, I wondered, "What must the people watching
me leave be thinking?" I was using a walker, wearing a surgical
shoe, and my eyes were dilated as I headed to the truck to drive
away.

A recent book added to the Overton Memorial Library was
written by "an ordinary professor of Old Testament studies" at a
German university. Turns out that "ordinary" isn't really ordinary. In the German system of ranking professors, an "ordinary
professor" ranks between a professor and an extraordinary professor. You can google it. Who would have guessed?

I have been asked, "Are you a complete idiot?" I was more
amused and perplexed than insulted. I'm certainly not a "complete" idiot. I have not yet done all the dumb things that I'm going
to do. And, just like a stopped watch is correct twice a day, I occasionally get some things right.

A past counseling referral was most interesting. The caller
said, "I don't know if you can help these people. They're really
old. I mean, they're in their 50s." I suddenly felt ancient. The
young have no clue how young they are.

I recently received some ten sets of assignments from a graduate course. Each set was strong and helpful. Because they were so well done, I could read them efficiently with joy. I think I learned something from every set. And then I got to send a complimentary email to each student. Talk about a win-win scenario (Heb 10:24).

On a recent Wednesday night, I was more tired than usual. We began our class from Jeremiah 1 and thoughtful comments poured in from the group. I found myself being educated. The atmosphere of learning put energy into the room. What I expected to be a bit disappointing because of my fatigue was transformed into a major blessing. God can do so much with the little that we bring to the table (Luke 17:5–6).

I was in the left lane preparing to turn into our neighborhood. I was driving at the speed limit when an impatient driver almost tapped my rear bumper. I was in his way. In a poor moment, I thought about locking my brakes and letting him smite me. Rejecting that vengeful plan, I made my turn and went home. Other people's errors need not lead us to err. Other people's issues need not cause us pain. Doing right can be its own reward (Rom 12:14–21).

I recently found myself at a lunch table with a friend who loves to talk—and needed to talk. I have big ears and wasn't pressed for time. I think we both were blessed. It's good to be good to others. It's more blessed to give than to receive. It does no harm to act better than you have to. God has set laws of sowing and reaping in place. Next time, I might be the one needing to talk. There are times when we just need to chill and let the moment be what it is (Jam 1:19).

Unexpected Answers

And Jesus said to him, "I will come and heal him." The centurion answered and said, "Lord, I am not worthy that You should come under my roof. But only speak a word, and my servant will be healed."

Matthew 8:7–8

Upon hearing that the little boy was five years old, his new adult friend asked, "And when will you be six?" "On my birthday!" came the classic, correct, and surprising answer.

A new student wanted to be advised for fall registration. I asked him, "How many hours are you thinking of taking?" His unexpected answer, "The catalog says I need 128." That is what the catalog says, but no one so far has taken the entire four-year course load in a single semester. We never even dreamed of offering the entire four-year curriculum in one semester.

At a local restaurant, I often get my fish blackened. Recently I asked, "Could I get that blackened?" The server replied, "We don't do that here." Policy had not changed; the server just didn't know that blackened was an option. Still that response beats the server who once asked, "You want it burned?" Reminds me of the famous adage: we don't know what we don't know.

Ask about football loyalties in Alabama, and you'll usually get either a crimson or an orange-and-blue response. Yet, I've heard a few people respond, "I don't really follow football." It always makes me wonder if they might be from another planet.

The Bible is full of unexpected answers:

- Adam begins the list when he tries to throw Eve under the bus in Genesis 3:12. His response could not possibly have yielded a positive outcome.

- Moses surprises us in Exodus 4:13 when he tells God, "Please send by the hand of whomever else You may send." Bottom line: "Pick anyone but me. You are mistaken. I am not your man!"

- Aaron's outright and outrageous lie from Exodus 32 continues to amaze us. "In went the gold, and out jumped a golden calf." Even a five-year-old wouldn't buy that story.

- We find the answer foretold by Jesus in Matthew 7:22 stunningly fearsome. Some who think that they have done great things in God's name will hear God say in judgment, "I never knew you; depart from Me, you who practice lawlessness!" God can't be fooled.

- On the positive side of unexpected answers, we love the answer given by the father of the prodigal son. He interrupts his son's confession of unworthiness to declare his joy and order a celebration. "He who was lost is found!" (Luke 15). Salvation is always joyous.

- In 1 Kings 21, we get a double dose of surprising responses. When God sends Ahab word of his impending doom, Ahab responds by humbling himself with fasting and mourning. I never would have guessed. And God responded by delaying His judgment of Ahab! Pure grace.

We love Samuel's all-time famous answer to the voice of God. "Speak, for your servant hears" (1 Sam 3:10). What a response! It shows humility, respect, willingness, and wisdom. It sets a wonderful example for us. It's always right to say yes to God.

People Are Fascinating

So then, my beloved brethren, let every man be swift to hear, slow to speak, slow to wrath.

James 1:19

A recent wait in a doctor's office provided plenty of opportunity for people watching. All this medical stuff is supposed to be confidential—I know because I had to sign forms allowing my other doctors to share records with the new one, forms allowing the doctor to talk to Laura in case of a health emergency, and forms allowing the doctor to send me emails or leave text messages on my phone. All that protection, and the receptionist asked me whatever she pleased within earshot of the entire waiting room. I'm glad I enjoy irony—it's everywhere.

Among those waiting was a saintly mother and her three-year-old daughter. It was no place for children—small, full, and boring. The poor kid had energy to burn. And her mom showed great patience and interest. I was reminded of how GREAT good moms are.

The office was having telephone issues. During the ninety-minute wait, I heard the receptionist explain that to person after person. Some of the callers had to hear it three times. That's so human. It's hard to tell any of us what we don't want to hear. Hearing odd news over and over doesn't make it a bit less odd. The truth is the truth—facts don't change because they're inconvenient. Most of us need to keep working on our application of James 1:19.

A woman came by needing paperwork that the office couldn't provide. I thought the receptionist's explanation made sense. I thought the same about the nurse's explanation and the doctor's explanation. The needy lady got loud; then, she got sarcastic. Sarcasm doesn't typically endear you to people in these sorts of situations. Loud sarcasm gets OBNOXIOUS in a hurry. I found myself wondering, "Why didn't she try being nice first?" Just ask.

Explain how you need help and how grateful you'd be to get it. Her parting words really left me perplexed. After all the negativity, she left with, "God bless you. Have a nice day." In truth God blessed us all when He let her leave, but that wasn't what she meant. God would have been more honored if she had never mentioned Him. Note to self: Remember her example, and don't follow it. It doesn't fit Ephesians 4:29–32. It's sad when you improve a room by leaving it.

I knew it was my turn to see the doctor when I was the only one remaining in the waiting room. I had read the counseling journal that I brought, watched people until I gave out, and viewed an episode of a soap opera for the first time in years. I also counted both the ceiling and the floor tiles—twice. I almost reached the point of reading one of the magazines on the table. I'm better at waiting than I used to be, but not much better. I'm still working on Ecclesiastes 7:8–9, "The end of a thing is better than its beginning. The patient in spirit is better than the proud in spirit. Do not hasten in your spirit to be angry, for anger rests in the bosom of fools."

It occurs to me that we often think we're waiting on God. In some senses we do, but I'm tremendously amazed at God's patience in waiting on us. God is not the one trying to figure things out and get things together. He's already there and working tirelessly to help us catch up. He's better to us than we'll ever know.

Ugly in Action

But avoid foolish and ignorant disputes, knowing that they generate strife. And a servant of the Lord must not quarrel but be gentle to all, able to teach, patient.

2 Timothy 2:23–24

I was third in line at a thrift store, but a crisis was holding us up. The man at the counter had made an unhappy $1 purchase. He decided not to want a small dish, and he demanded 50 cents back. Trouble was that store policy is "No Refunds, No Returns." It's on the sign, plain as day.

The more this fellow demanded the refund, based on the irrelevant fact that he had not taken the merchandise outside the store, the louder the clerk read him the policy. By this time, there was a line of seven potential customers. One lady put her item back on the shelf in order to escape.

Often, I'm not nearly as bright as I should be. It's clear the dispute was over 50 cents. The irate customer demanded to see the manager. There was no manager, only a second clerk. This made him even madder. I pulled two quarters out of my pocket and said to the clerks, "It's just 50 cents. I'm happy to fix this." As you might guess, the irate customer vetoed that approach. He wanted HIS 50 cents out of the register. You could have cut the negativity with a knife.

The clerks finally agreed to give the man his quarters, but the register wouldn't open until the next purchase was tallied. The crisis deepened. The angry man took offense at the notion of waiting while another customer was served. It was HIS TURN. And he refused to hear the clerks explain, for the fourth time, that the register could not be opened immediately.

Finally, the clerks prevailed, the man got two quarters, and he left. I either could not or would not (sometimes I'm not sure which) resist saying to the highly frustrated clerk, "You were right the whole time. Some people just won't let you be right."

Bless her heart, I don't think my comment helped her at all. Her day had suffered major damage.

Of course, the irate customer thought he was correct. Upon reflection, I believe he thought he was defending his rights and standing on principle. But he was factually, functionally, and attitudinally wrong. The store has the right to set its own policy. Just respect the rules.

Upon additional reflection, I see this whole episode as providential. God still works in mysterious ways. The Lord was teaching my fellow victims and me several important lessons:

- What made this man so sure that he was right and the clerk was wrong? Why am I sometimes just as wrongly certain as he was? Why couldn't he take a step back and consider the other person's point (Prov 16:25)?

- I'm glad my family and friends don't share that man's attitude. I don't think this was his first public rudeness—or his last. It would be stunningly frustrating to deal with him day by day (Prov 22:24–25).

- When tempted to be a jerk, fight that temptation. Don't give in (Jam 4:5–7).

- When given an opportunity to be nice, be nice. Cultivate kindness (2 Tim 2:23–26).

- Some fights aren't worth having. Odds are very low that your life is going to be harmed by paying an extra 50 cents in a thrift store. Why press a point that's not worth pressing, where even if you win, you lose (1 Cor 6:1–8)?

It's tragic to fail to consider the effect of our actions on others. Why berate the poor clerks? In what reality can it be good to make seven people wait and witness major verbal unpleasantness over mere pennies (Phil 2:3–4)?

Thoughts on "Normal"

Not everyone who says to Me, "Lord, Lord," shall enter the kingdom of heaven, but he who does the will of My Father in heaven. Many will say to Me in that day, "Lord, Lord, have we not prophesied in Your name, cast out demons in Your name, and done many wonders in Your name?"

Matthew 7:21–22

Patsy Clairmont wrote the book, *Normal Is Just a Setting on Your Dryer*. Very smart writer. Normal is highly over-rated and sometimes super boring.

I like the Chinese curse, "May you live in interesting times." (Are you allowed to like a curse?) Though it's difficult to define, most of us need a degree of normal. Things get tough when all of life moves faster than our comprehension and/or our ability to adjust. A degree of stability and predictability is a blessing. Without a degree of normality, it's hard to keep a job or a friendship.

We recognize the strong tendency to define "normal" from our personal experience and perspective. "Normal" is what's "normal" for me, no matter how odd that might be to others. For me, normal includes mayo on a banana sandwich and apple jelly (never grape) on a PB&J. Normal means no onions, no celery, and no chicken. I doubt that's true for most of you.

Recognizing our abnormalities can be challenging, depressing, developmental, fun, liberating, and scary. As you'd expect, I like that—it's one of the ways I'm abnormal. Beware of people who claim to be perfectly normal. Chances are they'll lie about other things as well.

In a sense, normal equals ordinary. Given our God-given uniqueness and potential, why would anyone settle for ordinary? I love people who give themselves permission to be different. I'm not talking about disrespecting God or people, just living creatively within God's rules. I put the faith-filled centurion of

Matthew 8:8–9 and the generous woman of Mark 12:41–44 in this group.

Practically, normal equals functional or capable. We wouldn't speak a word against that, unless it includes settling for merely functional and never aiming higher. Virtually all people have within them a capacity for greatness in some sense or situation. It's part of being made in the image of God. To rise above the normal and claim that gift or moment is anything but normal. We see Peter do that in Matthew 14:28, 16:16, and Luke 5:8.

Statistically, normal might be defined in terms of the number of standard deviations from the mean. While factual, that statement may not mean much. If we could create a scale, the most loving people around us would fall way out on the edge of our Bell Curve—and we'd be great with that. Much depends on which mean we're deviating from and the direction of the deviation. God is honored with our "abounding more and more" in any virtue (1 Thess 4:9–10; John 13:34–35; 2 Pet 1:5–8).

Sociologically, normal might be defined in terms of staying in step with the community around us. We know to be careful here. We don't want temporary marriages even if most around us divorce. We don't want to follow the god of materialism even if our culture loves him. We reject "Me first" and "My first duty is to myself" in favor of Matthew 16:24–26 and 22:34–40.

Religiously, normal might be defined in terms of Matthew 7:21–23 (hearing but not doing, serving self rather than God). Matthew 15:1–10 and Luke 13:1–5 also come into play. It's so easy to think that if we're just about as good as most folks (normal), then we're okay. We love all things good, but there is no salvation short of loving submission to Jesus.

Memorable Incompetence

Do not be wise in your own opinion.

Romans 12:16b

My errors had reached a new level. I was shopping for books at a local bargain store just after New Year's Day a few years back. One of the clerks approached me with a question: "Are you the one who recently bought a bunch of books here?" I was. "You left four of them here. I have them for you at the register." I wasn't even tempted to argue with her.

Somehow four of the books from the previous purchase had failed to make it into my buggy. It was very nice of them to hold the items. I would never have known.

Makes me wonder what else I don't know, realize, and/or remember. Makes me appreciate the ethics of the store's staff. Makes me all the more willing to welcome and appreciate help and other reminders from you. My need is right obvious.

There are many forms of poor reasoning and poor performance. I think of those drivers who try to traverse floodwaters. If you can't see the pavement, you don't know that it's still there. I think of myself trying to discern the instructions at the pump of an unfamiliar service station. If there's a wrong way to try, I can find it. I'm unskilled at basic card swiping. What seems intuitive to me never seems to work. I once ordered chicken at a German restaurant—I don't eat chicken when I can help it.

It's obvious that I'm living proof of Proverbs 21:2: "Every way of a man is right in his own eyes, but the Lord weighs the hearts." Proverbs 16:2 says almost the same thing. I'm glad the Lord can take motives and capacities into account. At the same time, however, I try hard to stay out of the first part of Proverbs 12:15, "The way of a fool is right in his own eyes, but he who heeds counsel is wise." I love the second part of the verse. I have no doubt that I often need both wise counsel and additional assistance.

One of the books that I found on the last trip to the bargain store was *Unusually Stupid Americans: A Compendium of All-American Stupidity*. I wish I could say that I bought it to see if I was included, but I have no such stature. Being non-famous has many advantages. Upon reflection, I think I bought it to remind me of our human commonality. Everybody falls into memorable incompetence at times. Seventeenth century English writer and politician, George Savile, once put it this way: "The vanity of teaching often tempteth a Man to forget he is a Blockhead." In the context of the quote, I'm a natural-born teacher.

If you see me looking for my truck, aim me toward it. If I leave it running, ask me if that was intentional. If you think I should be carrying an umbrella, suggest that I consider it. When you find my umbrella, please bring it back to me. If I fail to thank you, remind me that I promised to be better than that.

There are two cool things about memorable incompetence. First, it's anti-pride, and we all know what pride does (Prov 16:18). Plus, it helps us love Matthew 7:12 and Romans 12:10, 16. "Do not be wise in your own opinion" remains stunningly solid.

Righteous Rebellion

*And do not be conformed to this world, but be transformed
by the renewing of your mind, that you may prove what is that
good and acceptable and perfect will of God.*

Romans 12:2

I enjoy irony, oxymorons, and other figures of speech. They invite investigation. They require reflection. They entertain as they educate.

Righteous rebellion is an oxymoron, much like *jumbo shrimp*, where the two words seem contradictory. We know the devastating negativity of spiritual rebellion. Psalm 95:8 warns, "Do not harden your hearts, as in the rebellion" and is repeated in both Hebrews 3:8 and 15. Proverbs 17:11 reads, "An evil man seeks only rebellion; therefore a cruel messenger will be sent against him." Spiritual rebellion always leads to condemnation.

Righteous rebellion is a different concept. It's a way of obeying both Romans 12:2 and Colossians 3:1–2. It invites us to think outside this world's box as we set our minds on the things of God. We offer the following examples of righteous rebellion:

- Rebel against the pettiness of this world by honoring Matthew 22:37-38: "Jesus said to him, 'You shall love the Lord your God with all your heart, with all your soul, and with all your mind. This is the first and great commandment.'"

- Rebel against the arrogance of this world by honoring Proverbs 1:7 and 9:10: "The fear of the Lord is the beginning of knowledge" and "The fear of the Lord is the beginning of wisdom."

- Rebel against the egotism of this world by honoring Philippians 2:3–4: "Let nothing be done through selfish ambition or conceit, but in lowliness of mind let each esteem others better than himself. Let each of you look out not only for his own interests, but also for the interests of others."

- Rebel against the cruelty of this world by honoring John 13:34–35: "A new commandment I give to you that you love one another; as I have loved you, that you also love one another. By this all will know that you are My disciples, if you love one another."

- Rebel against the negativity of this world by honoring Philippians 2:14: "Do all things without complaining and disputing."

- Rebel against the worry of this world by honoring Matthew 6:33: "But seek first the kingdom of God and His righteousness, and all these things shall be added to you."

- Rebel against the doubt of this world by honoring 1 Peter 3:15: "But sanctify the Lord God in your hearts, and always be ready to give a defense to everyone who asks you a reason for the hope that is in you, with meekness and fear."

Choice and Perfect Irony

The entirety of Your word is truth, and every one of Your righteous judgments endures forever.

Psalm 119:160

I think it calls itself an antique mall, but it's more on the junk, stuff, and weirdness side of life. It's a cool place to plunder. One of the displays has three sections, each with multiple items. From each section, you could have your choice of items for $5.99, $8.88, or $12.99 respectively. And each little sign had a different spelling of choice: *chois*, *choise*, and *choice*. I took photos. I love the irony of being able to choose both an item and a spelling.

Of course, there's only one correct spelling of choice within standard English. What's up with the side-by-side-by-side inconsistency?

- Language purists see two errors and one case of accuracy.

- Pragmatists see no errors. All three signs communicate the intended message. And you wouldn't get a discount for noticing the abnormal spellings.

- Realists might think that the misspellings were intentional in an "I made you look" sort of way. They might be right; it worked on me.

- Humorists might view it as pleasantly intentional. The signs remind us all that life is full of quirky moments. Why leave such odd moments to chance; why not create some?

- Non-conformists would see a fellow free spirit (aka rebel) at work. Why conform to societal expectations? Why comply? Why not assert your freedom of expression?

- Logicians might see a powerful object lesson. There are always multiple ways to be wrong, imprecise, or inaccurate.

- Those who excel in gratitude might see it as a reminder to thank their best elementary teachers. "I knew the errors when I saw them, and I could pick the right option."

- The arrogant might find one more occasion to feel superior. "I don't make such silly errors. I'm better than that."

- Life-long learners will be moved to ask, "What lessons do these signs have for me?"

- Story-tellers will immediately start thinking, "How can I share this neat discovery?"

- The humble might think, "There but by the grace of God go I."

- Multi-modalists might see all of the above and more.

Fun little choices make pleasant diversions. Harmless little errors make us smile. The freedom to choose is a huge responsibility. Choosing to notice "the little things" opens doors for learning. Choosing excellence powerfully shapes our character. Choosing God and godliness both shapes our character and determines our destiny (Josh 24:15; Rom 5:1–5; 2 Pet 1:2–8).

Sweet Reminders

I will meditate on Your precepts, and contemplate Your ways. I will delight myself in Your statutes; I will not forget Your word.

Psalm 119:15–16

A student recently did excellent work on a major paper, but there were a few stylistic "variations." We sent him a list of requested corrections, and he sent us a sweet thank you for helping him improve his work. We love seeing such excellence in attitude and love for learning. Reminds us of Philippians 2:1–5 and 1 Corinthians 13:4–8.

A stranger appeared on campus, asking a favor. He had mechanical problems and wanted our permission to leave his car in our parking lot overnight. Here's a guy on a tough day going the second mile to be courteous. Reminds us of Matthew 5:41.

Our favorite delivery guy from UPS is always pleasant. If he has a large item or several items, he asks us where to put them. He doesn't have to do that, but he wants to be kind. Reminds us of Philippians 2:3–4.

A jail escapee recently triggered a lock-down on the HCU campus. Florence police were polite, attentive, and professional. That's been our consistent experience with FPD. Reminds us to appreciate Romans 13:1–7.

We recently visited a local antique store. It's the kind where people rent space to sell their wares. I found an African tribal mask in one of the booths, but it had no price. When we took it to the counter for payment, the clerk put it in a bag and said, "It's yours. I told them to put a price on everything or we'd give it away." Reminds me of both Numbers 32:23b and Proverbs 24:26.

We can offer no details out of respect for privacy, but some of the recent HCU graduates overcame tremendous trials to earn their degrees. Most people would have surrendered to the health issues, family struggles, or other challenges. It was a HUGE JOY to see their victory. Reminds us of Colossians 3:17 and 23–24.

I was trimming shrubs a few weeks ago when a black SUV stopped in the middle of the street. A lady exited holding a puppy. "Is this your dog? Have you seen him before? We found him in the street, and we're looking for his owner." I had never seen the dog or the lady before, but I appreciated her kindness and effort. Reminds me of Matthew 7:12.

We have several friends who have been rudely kicked around by life. They seldom feel well due to health issues, but they are consistently encouraging and optimistic. We can't be around them without being humbled and feeling blessed. It's wonderful to see such strong faith. The only explanation is that God lives in their hearts. They remind us of Philippians 4:10–13.

A local congregation needed a replacement speaker for a lesson on anxiety and depression. When their preacher called to ask me about filling in, he resisted the obvious temptation to say, "When I think of anxiety and depression, you're the first person who comes to mind." I appreciate his restraint. Sometimes what we don't say speaks volumes. Reminds me of Proverbs 25:11–12 and Ecclesiastes 3:7b.

Sweet reminders abound when we're willing to look. God is always seeking to bless us.

Strange Thoughts

Whoever guards his mouth and tongue keeps his soul from troubles.

Proverbs 21:23

O n Valentine's Day, I received an email greeting from a counseling group's "Do Not Reply" address. I love that. To me it says, "I'll be your Valentine so long as we don't have to interact." Way too many guys already think that way. It seems to say, "I love you, but let's not talk ever."

A friend at work came to the lobby to find his package. He received a message saying that it had been delivered. No package. Ten minutes later, we got a delivery, but his package was absent. We shouldn't believe everything that we read from the screen. Always check your sources.

An important event was advertised for Tuesday, February 19. That caused some confusion because February 19 is a Monday. Happens to the best of folks. Glad it wasn't me this time, but it sure sounds like something I would do. "He who is without sin among you, let him throw a stone at her first" (John 8:7). Matthew 7:1–4 fits just as well.

A university document tried to explain that the school maintains a healthy learning environment. What it said was, "HCU maintains a healthy leaning environment." I'm the person who omitted the "r." Now I want a photo of our people leaning notably. Maybe we could include a photo of that tower in Pisa. Reminds me of the sign-up sheet I created way back when for people to bring "deserts" to a gathering. I got drawings of cacti and sand dunes. Amazing how much difference a single letter can make. What we think we say often doesn't match what we really say.

One of my recurring dreams has reached "familiar old friend" status. I'm at a distorted version of my parents' house trying to clean up debris from the lawn and adjacent pastures. The harder I work, the more the piles of debris multiply. During the whole dream I "progress backwards," as Yogi Berra might have said. No one needs a guide to dreams to interpret this one. The meaning is just as obvious as it seems. The part I can't figure out is why I keep trying so hard. In other words, when you're going in the wrong direction, turn around; when what you're doing isn't working, try something else. Persistence is a virtue, but stubbornness is a vice.

I recently read a passionate letter from a person trying to correct what he saw as a major error. Sadly, he did not realize that the situation was much more complicated and nuanced than he had assumed. No one was trying to do wrong. There was no ill will or evil intent. Good people were looking at the same situation from radically different perspectives. Reminds us of Romans 14 and the divine appeal that we reject the temptation to despise our brethren (v. 3), leave judgments in matters of opinion to Christ (v. 10), and realize that "each of us shall give account of himself to God" (v. 12).

Heard of a guy who asked the clerk in the antique store, "How much is that clock in the window?" The reply, "Why? Do you want to buy it?" The retort, "No. I just love to ask people the price of clocks." It's a store. You want to sell things. Make it easy for people to buy them. Aggravating potential customers isn't a winning strategy. When people are headed in a good direction, don't get in their way. Make it easy for people to do the right thing. Those same principles apply to sharing the gospel and to every good work.

Contradictions

They profess to know God, but in works they deny Him, being abominable, disobedient, and disqualified for every good work.

Titus 1:16

I enjoy amusing and harmless contradictions. On the musical front, think of the song "Oh Susanna." "It rained so hard the day I left; the weather it was dry. The sun so hot I froze to death. Susanna don't you cry."

On the culinary side, we have jumbo shrimp and small drinks that are huge. And there's the guy who ordered his vegan entrée with extra bacon.

From a holiday perspective, there are people who'll wish you a stress-free Christmas, as if that were possible. As kids on the farm, we were told that Labor Day was for city people. It was a day for folks like us to work extra hard.

From a metaphorical viewpoint, do you know people who are as calm as a racehorse in the starting gate and as peaceful as a wounded Klingon?

I enjoy amusing and harmless contradictions, but I hate the other kind. I hate to see anything advertised as "no obligation, just sign the following contract." If there's no obligation, there's no contract to sign. I hate to hear politicians promise to increase services as they decrease taxes. Life doesn't work that way. I hate to hear preachers beg for funding while wearing Rolex watches and designer suits. I hate to hear preachers beg for money, period.

I lament the anti-education statement: "I don't need no education. I already know more than I can do." It's bad grammar and worse reasoning. I lament seeing heavy people going back for thirds in the buffet line. I especially hate that when it's me. I lament seeing kids trying to look tough or cool by inhaling a known carcinogen that causes everything from bad breath to hardening of the arteries. I hate to see people drink an addictive depressant and claim that it makes them happy.

And there are famous biblical contradictions:

- Think of those who call Him "Lord, Lord," but practice lawlessness (Matt 7:21–23).

- Think of those who honor God with lips, but their hearts are far from Him (Matt 15:8).

- Think of those who claim to love Jesus but have no use for His church (Matt 16:17–18; Eph 5:23–27).

- Think of those whose speech and actions do not match (Jam 2:14–16; 1 John 3:18).

- Think of those who claim to love God but hate their fellowman (1 John 4:11, 20).

We dare not deny Jesus through our words or our works (Titus 1:16). The hearts, lives, and teachings of Christians must be consistent with Scripture and congruent with Christ (Luke 6:40; Eph 4:11–16; Phil 2:5–11). Otherwise, we're just walking contradictions.

A Way With Words

*Unless Your law had been my delight, I would then have per-
ished in my affliction. I will never forget Your precepts, for by
them You have given me life.*

Psalm 119:92–93

Most of us enjoy wholesome wordplay and the pleasant turn of a phrase. At school we tend to have monthly snack and yak sessions. Some of us prefer chat and chew. I've even heard vittles and visits—we are decidedly southern.

I'm totally non-offended when some of my friends call the popular alternate worship schedule "church-eat-church." They know that it's actually worship-fellowship meal-worship, and they are not trying to deny biblical teaching. I have to smile when they say it too fast and it comes out "churchy-church" or when people hear the phrase like we're a bunch of cannibals.

We're often imprecise with our language in harmless ways. People still ask me, "How's your toe?" I often don't resist responding, "It's still gone." I know they're actually asking about my foot and my general well-being, but a little humor between friends seems okay.

I recently followed a stream of comments beneath an internet news story. One comment used the abbreviation *ppl*. In context, it translated into "people" to me. Others seemed utterly confused. Some of us truly need to have it all spelled out.

I stand amazed at how well God communicates with us through scripture. I can't imagine how difficult it is for the sinless and infinite to communicate with the finite and sinful. We don't even know our limitations in perspective and understanding.

Even given our weakness, don't you love the following sweet statements from scripture?

- "But as many as received Him, to them He gave the right to become children of God" (John 1:12).

- "There is therefore now no condemnation to those who are in Christ Jesus, who do not walk according to the flesh, but according to the Spirit" (Rom 8:1).

- "I will never leave you nor forsake you" (Heb 13:5 quoting Deut 31:6).

- "For it is God who works in you both to will and to do for His good pleasure" (Phil 2:13).

- "Be faithful until death and I will give you the crown of life." (Rev 2:10).

- "For we know that if our earthly house, this tent, is destroyed we have a building from God, a house not made with hands, eternal in the heavens" (2 Cor 5:1).

Add Psalm 23, John 14:1–4, Romans 5:8–6:8, 2 Corinthians 5:17, and other passages that lift your spirit. Our God has some way with words! We're blessed to hear Him always.

On Limits and Limitations

And now, Israel, what does the Lord your God require of you, but to fear the Lord your God, to walk in all His ways and to love Him, to serve the Lord your God with all your heart and with all your soul, and to keep the commandments of the Lord and His statutes which I command you today for your good?

Deuteronomy 10:12–13

One of the questions when I went to give blood recently was, "Have you been outside the country in the last three years?" I was just back from teaching in the Philippines. As the nurse struggled to find it in her manual, she asked me, "Is that a country? Does it have another name?" She had never heard of the Philippines and had no idea what Manila, a city of 14 million people, was.

I don't know if the American educational system failed this lady, if she failed it, or if the truth lies in some combination of those failures. It was a sad day.

Turns out that I'm deferred for a year from blood donations because of the low risk of malaria in rural regions of Luzon, the Philippine island on which I taught. It's a stunning example of the weakness of one-size-fits-all rules. Malaria is virtually non-existent on Luzon. I never saw or heard a mosquito. No one who visits Luzon on the mission teams that I know about ever takes antimalarials. Besides that, our visit was during the dry season, a time that's most unfriendly to mosquitoes.

Here's a rule that's meant to protect, but in reality, it keeps people from being helped. Human rules often do that. Colossians 2:20–23 and 1 Timothy 4:1–5 speak stoutly to this tendency.

While on campus at Asian Christian University, we met 22 of the cutest orphans ever. We inquired about the feasibility of American Christians being able to adopt any of them. Because of abuses in the past and bureaucratic realities, it's virtually impossible. If we understood correctly, in order to qualify for adoption, the prospective parents would be required to reside in the Philippines for two years. Most foreigners just can't do that.

I'm not anti-rule. One of my chief jobs at Heritage Christian University is enforcing our academic catalog and related educational best practices. When a sign says, "Keep off the grass," I do. The concept of "always challenge authority" strikes me as inefficient, annoying, and non-sensical.

That said, I admit that rules work best for me under the following conditions:

- When they're based in reality.
- When they're understandable.
- When they're open to discussion and improvement.
- When they're communicated clearly.
- When they're applied fairly.
- When they serve an important purpose.

My recent journeys and their unintended consequences remind me of the limitations of human rules, human logic, human wisdom, and human knowledge. Solomon and Jeremiah had it right. We need more help than we realize (Prov 14:12, 21:3; Jer 10:23).

Offers

I call heaven and earth as witnesses today against you, that I have set before you life and death, blessing and cursing; therefore choose life, that both you and your descendants may live.

Deuteronomy 30:19

I guess everyone who goes online gets offers of every type. Recently mine have included the following:

- Discounted liposuction. I won't be accepting for many reasons. Somewhere near the top is the question, "If I wanted liposuction would I really want the discount variety?" That has way too much potential for Murphy's Law to intervene.

- Anti-aging cream that will decrease my wrinkles. I'm very comfortable with my wrinkles, and the logic doesn't work. Even if I hid every wrinkle permanently, I'd still be just as old as I am.

- Offers to apply for various jobs in education and ministry. I think I'm what they call "fully employed." There's no wanderlust, and I can't get all my current work done.

- Offers to share my banking information with people offshore who will give me millions if I help them move their money. I don't even know my banking information; Laura handles all that. And even I wouldn't fall for those scams.

The world is constantly marketing its products. More than that, the world is constantly marketing its version of reality and its versions of success. Some of the products are OK, but the unbiblical versions of reality and success aren't. 1 John 2:15–17 comes to mind. We don't love the world because "if anyone loves the world, the love of the Father is not in him." We don't love the world because "all that is in the world ... is not of the Father." We don't love the world because "the world is passing away."

So much around us is hype and illusion, smoke and mirrors. "Buy this, and you'll be happy." "Go there, and you'll find peace." "Do this, and you'll feel the joy that has escaped you all of your life."

I prefer the better offers, the more realistic ones. If we stay in 1 John, the following come to mind:

- "But if we walk in the light as He is in the light, we have fellowship with one another, and the blood of Jesus Christ His Son cleanses us from all unrighteousness" (1:7).

- "If we confess our sins, He is faithful and just to forgive us our sins and to cleanse us from all unrighteousness" (1:9).

- "But whoever keeps His word, truly the love of God is perfected in Him. By this we know that we are in Him" (2:5).

- "Beloved, now we are children of God; and it has not yet been revealed what we shall be, but we know that when He is revealed, we shall be like Him, for we shall see Him as He is" (3:2).

- "For if our heart condemns us, God is greater than our heart, and knows all things" (3:20).

- "You are of God, little children, and have overcome them, because He who is in you is greater than he who is in the world" (4:4).

- "For whatever is born of God overcomes the world. And this is the victory that has overcome the world—our faith" (5:4).

- "And we know that He hears us, whatever we ask, we know that we have the petitions that we have asked of Him" (5:15).

What offers of grace, hope, and victory! And all of them come from God Himself.

Questions that Evoke Wonder

For who is God, except the Lord? And who is a rock, except our God?

Psalm 18:31

The unsolicited post proved engaging and helpful. It dealt with using insightful questions to increase motivation and engagement among college students. It did more than that for me.

On the level of college and university students, it made me wonder:

- What are they doing in school if they aren't motivated? Do I really want to know?

- Why just go through the motions? Why not engage and make the best of each class?

- When did it become a major part of the teacher's job to incite student motivation?

- Does the need for extrinsic motivation suddenly appear as students start college? Hardly. Laura sees that among sixth graders, but it starts even sooner.

My questions betray a bevy of assumptions. I believe that educational opportunities are a blessing. I believe students should bring the bulk of their own motivation. I believe that students should be creative enough to find some benefit in virtually any class. And I don't believe the buck should stop with just the teacher. Obviously, I believe many strange things.

I love the phrase "questions that evoke wonder." The Bible is full of them. The Psalms are particularly rich:

- *"Why do the nations rage, and the people plot a vain thing?" (Psa 2:1)* Do people really think they can effectively oppose God? Do they think spiritual rebellion is a war they can win?

- *"What is man that You are mindful of him, or the son of man that You visit him?" (Psa 8:4)* Why is God so good to us? Why do we continue to receive grace after mercy after blessing? Why do people who ought to know better present Psalm 8:4 as an accusation or a put down?

- *"Why do You stand afar off, O Lord? Why do You hide in times of trouble?" (Psa 10:1)* Why do we see rational answers to those ancient questions when they're applied to others, but go blind when we're the ones facing the trouble? Do we forget that God's time is not our time? Do we forget that premature deliverance thwarts spiritual growth? Do we forget that even our perception of time is relative and often errant?

- *"Lord, who may abide in Your tabernacle? Who may dwell in Your holy hill?" (Psa 15:1)* A perfect and challenging set of answers follows. Knowing those answers, why do we still struggle with our tongues, with basic honesty, and with materialism?

- *"Who can understand his errors?" (Psa 19:12)* We don't know what we don't know. We can't grasp perfection. We struggle with the concept of holiness. Can we grasp the wisdom of David's response to his own question? He both confesses and seeks forgiveness. On top of that, he asks for help to do better next time.

Unexpected Blessings

Now it shall come to pass, if you diligently obey the voice of the Lord your God, to observe carefully all His commandments which I command you today, that the Lord your God will set you high above all nations of the earth. And all these blessings shall come upon you and overtake you, because you obey the voice of the Lord your God.

Deuteronomy 28:1–2

Don't we love being surprised by God? An extra-brilliant rainbow. A double rainbow. A deer with its fawn. An antique car, or even better, an antique truck. A stunning sunset. A chance encounter with an old friend. Finding a new friend. Getting helped by a stranger. Seeing an old couple continuing to be sweet to one another. Whether subtle or overt, we love those moments.

On a day I thought to be busy, I left work for a hospital visit. It's strange that I thought of it that way. Ministry is our work—the work of every believer.

The gentleman I visited knew that I had come to check on him, but he immediately made it his business to check on me. He asked about mutual friends and the progress of the gospel. He "lit up" as I shared the latest good news from school and from church. He summoned energy that I didn't know he had to commend those works and to encourage continual progress. And he welcomed prayer just as prayer should be welcomed—as precious communion between God and friends. What a set of blessings!

I wouldn't call hospitals my favorite places to visit. One of the elevators was out of commission, and the other one was slow. It was raining a bit that day. I was tired and not at my best. But the effort offered blessings before, during, and after the visits.

- One of the volunteers at the front desk has the sweetest smile, and she's always pleasant.

- We waited extra for the elevator, but everyone who got on was pleasant and polite.

- After the visits, I found several helpful and almost free books for the Overton Memorial Library.

- And I found a cheap brass trumpet at a thrift store. It was meant to be a candleholder, but I'll never go that route. It has character, and it fits me. A horn that doesn't play for a guy who will never play a horn.

While I'm glad for the blessings I saw, I now wonder how many I missed. We tend to get busy and distracted—should we call it "dull of seeing" in the spirit of Hebrews 5:11? We'd be wise to ask God to open our eyes, our minds, and our hearts to see more of His constant goodness.

This world lives in darkness, and it loves the darkness (John 1:6–11 and 3:16–21). Yet God both is and offers constant light. How fitting that the darkest of Old Testament books offers these unexpected blessings: "Through the Lord's mercies we are not consumed, because His compassions fail not. They are new every morning: Great is Your faithfulness. The Lord is my portion, says my soul, therefore I will hope in Him" (Lam 3:22–24). Hope in the Lord opens the door for countless blessings, both the faithfully expected and stunningly surprising.

Minor Amusements

A merry heart does good, like medicine, but a broken spirit dries the bones.

Proverbs 17:22

I know that it doesn't take much to amuse me, and I'm happy with that. Being amused is generally better than being bored, angry, confused, frustrated, or disengaged. Several recent observations apply.

An email began, "I can't wait to meet you." Really? I don't belong on anybody's can't-wait-to-meet-you list. If a person doesn't even know me, how would he know that he can't wait to meet me? Of course, the now deleted email was just a solicitation.

The email that offered me a discount on liposuction was interesting. Talk about fishing in the wrong pond. On my worst day, I don't find lipo tempting. I don't think the results would impress me, and I'm way too old to try to impress others.

Speaking of fat, in some fast food restaurants they still ask me, "Do you want to supersize that?" It's a challenging question. The truest answer is, "Yes, I'd love to." The real answer is, "No, I'm already supersized enough." Same deal with, "Would you like fries with that?" What I want to do and what's best to do don't always match.

I cracked up at the recent TV commercial that included the line: "Change your bathtub, change your life." Not unless I slipped in the tub and broke something. I've never considered adding bathtubs to my list of life-changers, but don't you wish it could be that simple?

Then there's the commercial offering a lease on a convertible luxury car for some $700 per month. Now, that would change my life—not the car—but the consistent outflow of $700 per month. No offense to those who love convertibles, but I want my car to have a top. There's nothing about me that needs or wants a luxury car. I don't even mind that my truck's windows roll up and down with handles. But sometimes I wish the radio still worked.

In recent travels, we passed by a community called Lone Oak. I'm too literal for that. If the oak died, I'd want to change the name to No Oak. If other acorns sprouted, I'd be changing the name each spring—Two Oaks, Ten Oaks, etc. Eventually, I'd go hyperbolic and try Thousand Oaks, but I'd still hope that nobody else was counting the trees.

I mentioned Lone Oak to a friend who then asked me, "Have you heard of the community called No Hope?" I had not, but it gave me much reason to think. Was it named by someone with his tongue planted firmly in his cheek? (Is it possible to plant your tongue firmly in your cheek?) Was it named by someone who was battling major depression? Was it named by a follower of Nietzsche? Was it named by a person who really liked his little community, wanted it to stay small, and hoped the discouraging name would keep people away? So many possibilities.

If I lived in No Hope, I hope I'd move. No hope means no joy. Despite all the negatives in this sin-damaged world, there's still so much to enjoy. Choosing to see the joy in everyday life can help get us through the tough days. The wise man had it right, "A merry heart does good like medicine, but a broken spirit dries the bones" (Prov 17:22). Since God gives us the ability to choose our outlook, it doesn't make sense to live with dry bones.

Birthday Reflections

The days of our lives are seventy years; and if by reason of strength they are eighty years, yet their boast is only labor and sorrow; for it is soon cut off, and we fly away.

Psalm 90:10

Though it wasn't one of the infamous round numbers, a recent birthday provided incentive for reflection. It's smart to find a measure of joy in your birthday. Others do, and it makes no sense to let them have all the fun.

Birthdays are fine times for pleasant surprises. I loved one card in particular. It had a message from the National Foundation for Lowered Expectations. It read, "Have an Adequate Birthday." Irony, pragmatism, humor, and reality rolled into one simple card.

I was given a cane that has extra character. It came from an estate sale. It looks like something a witch would use to turn children into toads. In that I believe some children should be turned into toads, at least temporarily, I love that cane and the fantasies it inspires.

On the night before my birthday, I enjoyed one of my recurring dreams. Most of my recurring dreams are comforting—something like hearing a pleasant old story again. I'm back at my parents' home, walking up the hill toward Amma's house. (Amma was Grandmother Bagents. I was the first grandchild, couldn't say my "g," and she got stuck with Amma.) I start finding coins at the edge of the road. I keep finding and gathering coins. Even a BIG wreck by an 18-wheeler doesn't stop me from finding and gathering coins. When I woke up, my fingers hurt from all the gathering. I'm always a little disappointed that there are no coins.

There are some things we all should do on our birthday. Take some time off. Buy a gift for somebody else. Buy yourself an odd little gift. Make a visit to a pleasant friend. Thank God for another year. Tell God that you know you won't keep having these birthdays forever—and be sure you hear yourself telling Him that. Call and check on your parents—what a blessing to still have them around at my advancing age. Remember good times and good people. Think of heaven. Hold up the mirror of God's word and ask, "What do I need to fix? How do I need to grow? What do I need to stop, start, or otherwise change?" Be glad that many people still treat us better than we deserve and pray for those who don't. Remember favorite birthdays from the past—relive the memories as vividly as possible. Watch a favorite movie again. Read some happy pages from a new book. Tell some wonderful people that you love them. In my case, be happy that birthdays come still and that they only come once a year. Come to think of it, virtually all of those things would be good to do on any given day.

I know some good people who celebrate their half-birthdays. They mark the day that's six months from their birthday and declare it their half-birthday. I have no problem with that, but it would never work for me. Logically, I'd need to get half-cards and half-gifts. I'd need a half-cake with half-candles.

I know other good people who celebrate their spiritual birthdays. They celebrate the anniversary of the date that they were born again by being baptized into Christ (Acts 2:38; Rom 6:4–7; Gal 3:26–29). Now, there's a birthday worthy of continual celebration.

Can't Believe What
I Just Heard

He who answers a matter before he hears it, it is folly and shame to him.

Proverbs 18:13

I was recently told about two men whose connection stems from the fact that "they have the same birthday every year." I think I might have figured out the "every year" part.

The week before the annual reversion from daylight savings time, a friend heard a weathercaster say, "It'll be colder than usual tomorrow night as we'll have an extra hour of darkness." Does he really think that our adjustments of the clock affect the sun?

As I ordered my salad at the barbecue place, I asked for a side of hot slaw to dump on the salad. I realized I had given unnecessary information when the waitress immediately responded, "That's strange." She knows me.

Upon buying some twenty-five used books for the Overton Memorial Library, the gentleman at the desk asked me, "Do you need a box?" Actually it took two boxes. I guess I could have carried them out an armful at a time.

I found a nice red and black dead-blow hammer at Bargain Hunt. It has granules for weight to minimize recoil. It's the best conversation starter I have in my office. Favorite comments range from "Planning some destruction?" to "You seem to be having a bad day. Should I hide your hammer?" You can guess the answers.

When I'm asked, "How are you?" one of my favorite responses is, "I'm trying hard." I'm working on making that more consistently accurate. A second favorite response is, "I'm peaceful." I'm always happy when people find that amusing, but I often wonder why they do.

I have asked people, "How are you?" meaning to be polite and non-invasive, only to receive way more information than I ever expected. The range has been from major confessions to floods of painful retelling. From time to time, friends know they have a lot to tell, so when I ask, "How are you?" they reply, "Do you really want to know?" I want my consistent answer to be an honest, "Yes."

James 3 is just as true as the rest of scripture. Our words have tremendous power. Words have both started and ended wars. The same could be said of marriages, business partnerships, and friendships. Words can make hearers glow or bleed. They can make spirits soar or crash.

We're blessed to weigh our words. Do they flow from earthly wisdom or from "the wisdom that is from above" (Jam 3:17)? Are they gracious and "seasoned with salt" (Col 4:6)? Will they land in love or strike like a hammer? Might they sometimes even do both (Matt 16:23)?

We're blessed to measure our words. "A fool vents all his feelings, but a wise man holds them back" (Prov 29:11). "He who answers a matter before he hears it, it is folly and shame to him" (Prov 18:13). "He who has knowledge spares his words" (Prov 17:27). "In the multitude of words sin is not lacking" (Prov 10:19). It seems that our words need lots of measuring.

We're also blessed to show grace and good humor toward those whose words don't come out right. That would be every human who will ever live—except for the Perfect One (Jam 3:1–2; 1 Pet 2:22). Since I want people to hear me better than I speak, I need to show the same courtesy to them.

On Errors

Rebuke is more effective for a wise man than a hundred blows on a fool.

Proverbs 17:10

I don't like errors, especially the ones that I make. But I have learned to find little errors amusing. Recently I've seen the following in newspapers:

- "Milllions" looks funny with the third "l."

- An article on flooding in Indonesia shouldn't be head-lined, "Floods in India."

- The mast of "Section C" shouldn't tell you to look for articles in "Section D" when there is no "Section D."

I heard a sportscaster read about a player "returning back" to his former team. "Returning" takes care of "back." I heard a friend ask of someone, "Where is he at?" "Where is he?" works just fine. It's a bit like the cowboy who said of his hopelessly injured horse, "I shot him dead and killed him." Twice evidently, and that's hard to do. In my first draft of this article, I typed "fiend" rather than friend when quoting Proverbs 27:17 in the last paragraph! And I don't even like the concept of frenemies.

Working with a university and being married to an English teacher, I'm trained to notice errors. That's not really a problem unless I begin to enjoy noticing them. It's even OK to help people correct errors, provided that I work on my own first (Matt 7:1–6) and keep my attitude and motives right (Gal 6:1–2).

It has been well said, "Only the dead make no errors." In one sense, errors are evidence of effort. We'd rather make—and cor-rect—errors than to let fear keep us from trying. The infamous "one talent man" of Matthew 25 didn't fare so well.

Errors provide opportunity for the devil. He will tempt us to pride and defensiveness when others notice our mistakes. He'll tempt us toward lies and excuses. He'll invite us to impugn the motives of good people who try to help us improve.

Errors also provide opportunity for the Lord. He corrects or chastens everyone whom He loves (Heb 12:3–11). He does so "for our profit." He does so to move us toward righteousness. And, often, He uses the people around us to point out our need to improve. It wouldn't be wise to oppose someone who is doing the Lord's work.

When you try to help me improve, I hope I'll know that—by your tone and your wisdom (Prov 15:1). When you try to help me improve, I hope I'll appreciate that—and say so—not just with words, but also by doing better. Isn't that the point of Proverbs 27:17? "As iron sharpens iron, so a man sharpens the countenance of his friend." Friends help friends improve. It's spiritually and relationally unwise and off-putting to be difficult to correct (Prov 12:15; 15:12; 17:10). May the Lord bless us to remember that we all need all the help that the Lord sends.

Contact Precautions

Pure and undefiled religion before God and the Father is this: to visit orphans and widows in their trouble, and to keep oneself unspotted from the world.

James 1:27

Because of his depressed immune system, everybody who entered my son Allen's cubicle in MICU had to wear a gown, mask, and gloves. Twice on each side of his door and once on the computer screen, the tape repeated, "CONTACT PRECAUTIONS." Those signs made me think that some people need that label for spiritual rather than medical reasons.

Gossips need the "Contact Precautions" sign. The enemies of Jesus and Paul used gossip against them. Proverbs 16:28 reminds us that "a whisperer separates the best of friends." If gossips can do that to friends, what must they be able to do to strangers and enemies! Many of them are so skilled at their craft. For a while, they can make you think that they actually care about truth and the people they are assassinating with their words.

Chronically critical people need the sign. For them even God's kindest blessings are a setup for pain. The sun is for sunburn, and the rain is for floods. Food is for food poisoning. All compliments are flattery and manipulation. All invitations hide a hook. Their dark view of the world can discourage even the finest of saints (Eph 4:29–32; Titus 3).

Perpetually angry people need the sign. "Make no friendship with an angry man, and with a furious man do not go, lest you learn his ways and set a snare for your soul" (Prov 22:24–25). Those who are perpetually angry train their eyes to see the worst and their hearts to hate. Like the hyper-critical, their senses are skilled at confirming their mindset.

Rebellious people need the sign. Some rebel specifically against God and His church. Others rebel against authority in most any form—government, parents, leaders, rules, and more.

They delight in being self-willed. To the inexperienced, they often look cool and free. That's not how they look to God (Rom 6:16; 2 Tim 3:1–9).

Lazy people need the "Contact Precautions" sign. We know what a low view the Proverbs take of laziness (6:6–11; 10:4; 12:24; 13:4). In contrast, we know what a high view the entire Bible takes of work (Eph 4:28; Col 3:22–24). We know what happened to the one-talent man who did nothing to serve his master. And we know that laziness can be highly contagious. Few things demotivate workers like seeing their peers doing nothing.

Regrettably, dangerous people and dangerous situations don't come with warning labels. And that's only half the story. Even the best and wisest of us aren't always wise. Each of us is fragile and vulnerable in certain ways at certain times under certain conditions. Peter was certain that he'd never deny Jesus. I doubt Barnabas ever dreamed that he would discourage some brethren under pressure from others (Gal 2:13).

How wise for us to use spiritual contact precautions! We must remain sober, prayerful, and vigilant. Pleasing God demands remaining unspotted from the world (Jam 1:27).

Enjoying the Odd

Then Moses said, "I will now turn aside and see this great sight, why the bush does not burn."

Exodus 3:3

I realize that I over-enjoy the odd. To the best of my knowledge, that habit does no harm. Plus, it's free and fun.

Whether the spam filter catches them or not, we all get garbage emails. I reached a new low in garbage emails recently. It was an invitation to participate in a webinar on "exothermic reactions in landfills." Oh, the irony!

The same day, there was another email wanting me to buy a book on contextualized Christology in northeastern India. I could not decide if my favorite chapter was "Indigenous Theology as Postcolonial Theology" or "Situating Naga-Indigenous Theology." I consider them equally beyond my ability to understand. Even I am not odd enough to want to read those chapters.

I must admit that I certainly don't enjoy everything odd. As much as I appreciate irony, I can neither enjoy nor understand protestors who hang and burn people in effigy while claiming to oppose hate and promote love. I don't see violence promoting peace, yelling profanity promoting healthy communication, or vandalism promoting civility.

God understands our attraction for the odd. Remember how He gained the attention of Moses and piqued his curiosity with a bush that burned and yet was not consumed (Exod 3)? What a way to set up a meeting! God chose to amaze Moses before commissioning him as leader of the exodus. Could that be one reason we resist God's commission today—even after every miracle in scripture plus the life and teaching of Jesus—is that we have not yet been amazed by God?

Of course, the burning bush isn't nearly the oddest story in scripture.

- We love it when the serpent Moses produces swallows the serpents produced by Pharaoh's magicians (Exod 7).

- We find it so perplexing that God would order the raising of a bronze serpent to stop a plague of serpents (Num 21). In the next chapter, a donkey speaks!

- I have always loved Elisha causing the borrowed ax head to float (2 Kings 6).

- We love the stunningly odd business of a hand—with no arm and no body—writing on the wall (Dan 5).

- Most of us remember the odd diet and clothing of John the Baptizer (Matt 3).

- In a strange way, we appreciate the odd and gross way that God delivered judgment on prideful King Herod (Acts 12).

- We love the unforeseen way that God transported Paul to preach in Rome (Acts 27).

It's amazing how God can use the odd to grab and keep our attention.

Contrarian Unbeliever

For as the heavens are higher than the earth, so are My ways higher than your ways, And My thoughts than your thoughts.

Isaiah 55:9

When it comes to predictions of bad weather, I'm what you might call a contrarian unbeliever. The higher the percentage for ice and snow, the less I believe it will come. When forecasters dropped the chances of wintry precipitation from 80% to 40% one February evening, I should have seen the travel problems coming.

We closed the university for the day due to the slick roads, but a few of us slid into campus anyway. It was fascinating to observe other drivers. Some strangely assumed that since there was snow, the traffic lights no longer mattered. Others thought that normal "dry road" speed was a good idea. Wiser (than me) people delayed their travel a bit.

I'm comfortable with my label of contrarian unbeliever when it comes to predictions of bad weather. Historically, doubting has served me well. In Alabama, we're blessed to escape bad weather far more often than we encounter it.

That said, I must confess that I have a role in making weather-related decisions for the Heritage Christian University campus. Ultimately individuals make their own safety choices, but we can make those decisions easier or more difficult. We know the principles to apply: Proverbs 16:25, 17:27–28, and 29:11; Matthew 7:12; Philippians 2:1-4. But we don't always know just how to apply them.

It would be woefully ignorant to think that bad things don't happen to good people. Abel, Naboth, Jesus, and the innocents of both Ramah and Bethlehem deny that lie.

It would be just as ignorant to think that every negative event is sent directly from God either to punish people or to wake us up. But I admit that Luke 13:1–5 makes me want to check my heart and soul when I hear of bad events, whether natural or man-made.

I find that I'm a contrarian unbeliever when it comes to many forms of technology and our dependence on it. On many days, I seem to be able to cause scanner malfunction just by standing in that line. PA and computer systems that have never before mal-functioned seem to delight in making me their exception to the rule.

Sometimes I think it's really bad to be a contrarian unbeliever, but it's really a middle-of-the-road position. We all know people who are pessimistic true believers. They are certain that if it can go wrong it will, sooner and more aggravatingly than anyone anticipated. It will go wrong, and it cannot be fixed.

No big problem if I doubt the weather forecast. If I get wet, I'll drip dry. With travel I'll use due caution and pray before I go. The big problem would come if I started over-estimating my knowledge or doubting God's. He knows, even if we think He doesn't. We often don't know, even if we're sure that we do. In ten minutes He can coat nature in a blanket of white. And in fewer than ten weeks, He will coat nature in a blanket of green. It's good for us to know that there's much we don't know.

I'm Not Insulted

Also do not take to heart everything people say, lest you hear your servant cursing you. For many times, also, your own heart has known that even you have cursed others.

Ecclesiastes 7:21–22

I'm what you might call late middle aged. I'm not insulted if you think I'm old and near death. Only the Lord knows. I'm not insulted if you call me "young man." Whether you describe me as young or old, I won't even try to figure out whether you're serious, joking, or otherwise. Even if we disagree, there's no value in pushing the point.

I've been to school, one way or another, for most of my life. I'm not insulted if you think I need help, ask me if I need help, or just help me. I'm going to assume the best about your effort as long as is feasible.

I was born and have lived all my life thus far in Alabama. I'm not insulted if you think I talk "funny" or slow. You're entitled to your opinion, even if it doesn't match mine. Variety can be pleasant, distracting, and educational.

I vote every time there's an election. I'm not insulted if you think that I'm affiliated with one party or another. I'm really a big-time independent. I'm not insulted if you think that's strange. There are much stranger aspects of my personality and behavior.

I'm an Auburn graduate and an Auburn fan. My first degree is in agronomy, the crops and soils version. Way back in the day, I voted for Bessie the Holstein for homecoming queen. Though never crowned, she won by a landslide. We even had campaign ad t-shirts. Her election was primarily a protest against the perceived pomposity of the campus social structure. But I'm not insulted if you think it's outrageous to have voted for a cow. Upon reflection, I've voted for far worse candidates.

I'm technologically illiterate. I'm not insulted if you know that or even if you assumed it. Social media have very little to entice me. I don't even want to need the latest gadgets. I know bright people who can help me maintain basic computer function. God bless them for being willing to help.

If you speak to me, I'm grateful. If you don't, I'm not insulted. I'm going to assume that you didn't see me, that you were lost in thought, or that you have more on your plate than you can handle. I don't and shouldn't expect to be center of your universe.

If you send me a birthday card on the wrong day of the wrong month, I'm not insulted. I'll thank you for trying, and I'll mean it. Being remembered is often better than being ignored.

If I'm not the center of your attention, I'm not insulted. I love to "people watch." I notably prefer that to being watched or feeling watched. But if you want to watch, no offense will be taken.

I hope I have learned not to wear my feelings on my sleeve. Hypersensitivity is not a blessing. As some have put it clearly and succinctly with so much of life, "It's not about you." Most people don't think of us nearly as frequently as we might imagine. I'm just happy to be here. Every day has more blessings than bothers, and whether I see that or not is largely my choice.

An upward, outward, and positive focus fits with Matthew 5:16, 6:33, and 7:12. It fits well with Matthew 22:34–40 and John 13:34–35. When we love the Lord and delight in His will, so many aspects of life become easier. We don't have to question our worth, our purpose, our destiny, or our identity. And when others do, we're not insulted. The way we view life, God's view trumps both theirs and ours (Rom 5:1–11; 8:31–39; 1 John 3:1–3, 20). To belong to God and be loved by Him has always been life's greatest honor. It remains the key to joy, hope, and peace.

Chilling Reminders

Jesus Christ is the same yesterday, today, and forever.

Hebrews 13:8

An afternoon one early February brought record warmth of 79 degrees. Just after daylight the next morning, it was 29. During that same day, we saw both brilliant sun and driving rain.

Recently I heard about a tornado that took down buildings in south Alabama that were described as "historic landmarks." The wind neither knew nor cared that they were old and treasured. They were here for over a hundred years and gone in an instant.

I still read the local newspaper for the comics and obituaries. There are often death notices of people younger than I am. Recently among eleven notices, four were younger than me. Upon hearing of a death, a friend said of the deceased, "I just talked with him two days ago!" I'm still not sure what I'm supposed to do with that remark.

Thus, our minds turn to the nature, rapidity, and inevitability of change.

- Many things change without our approval. Lamenting such changes may be natural, but adjusting to them is far more profitable (Rom 8:28; Phil 4:11–13).

- Many things change way faster than we thought possible (Luke 12:16–21). That should remind us of the limitations of our thinking. It should make us pay more attention to God.

- Change isn't always for the better (Eccles 12:1–5). Statements like "I love change!" need to be made and heard in context and with prayerful consideration. Without spiritual contextualization, such assertions are foolish and easily falsified.

- Because physical things change—they burn, blow up, blow away, move off, sink, or die—we're wise to appreciate the good ones today. Don't lament their departure in advance. Don't take them for granted. Treat every good moment as a gift from God (Jam 1:17).

- Change is inevitable, but intentional change is not. We get to choose to participate in God's efforts to make us more like Jesus (2 Pet 1:5–8).

- No physical change can hold a candle to the spiritual change that God works when He saves us. We keep the same physical body and more, but we get a new heart, a new mind, a new hope, a new joy, a new family, and a new purpose (2 Cor 5:14–19). God's ability to effect immediate, eternal positive change is amazing.

What will change today? Will I notice? Will I understand? How should I adjust to the changes I encounter? How will God be helping me? How can I change for the better today? Will I choose to move toward God today? How can I help others draw nearer to God? Does my hope rest fully on the unchanging God (Mal 3:6; Heb 13:8)?

Little Stick, Little Burn

Your word is a lamp to my feet and a light to my path.

Psalm 119:105

A recent medical test called for a bit of lidocaine before the procedure. The doctor's preparatory words were, "Little stick, little burn." I wish. It turned out to be little stick, impressive burn.

I should have expected that. My family tends to be medicinally unique. We often don't respond as anticipated. When Allen was in Johns Hopkins Hospital in Baltimore, the nurse would bring a medication and say, "This will make you sleepy." More often than not, the pills would "wire" him. When she said, "This may keep you awake," we generally counted on some hours of deep sleep.

Being medically unique, I should have learned by now to "expect the unexpected," as they say. I find that I'm not so good at that. I don't know that I'm really good even at expecting the expected. "The unexpected" covers infinite territory.

I'm impressed (but not positively), by the pharmaceutical commercials that include the line, "Don't take _____ if you are allergic to _____ or any of its ingredients." You think? Besides, I do not know whether I'm allergic to _____ unless I've had a negative reaction. I understand a bit about lawyers and liability. I wish they understood more about common sense versus nonsense.

Just as we may not know how certain medications will affect us, we often don't know how certain situations or interactions will affect us. Maybe it would be wise to anticipate and prepare to the degree that we are able. God's word offers great help.

With loud and angry people, we know to apply Proverbs 15:1. We turn our volume down and take a soft approach. We don't let others cause us to sin. We love peace-making (Matt 5:9).

With fearful and uncertain people, we remember the warning of Revelation 21:8 and the encouragement of Hebrews 10:19–25. Feeling fear isn't a sin but being paralyzed by fear is. Battling doubts won't destroy us but giving in to doubts will.

With lazy and apathetic people, we know to apply Colossians 3:22–24. We don't want to be harsh or unfair. At the same time, we know the Lord's low opinion of both laziness and apathy (Prov 10:26; Rev 3:15–16). The term "lazy Christian" is a terribly sad oxymoron.

With complaining or accusing people, we know to apply Philippians 2:3–4. We listen politely and do our best to understand their perspective. We seek win-win options where love and respect prevail. If that fails, we apply Romans 12:18. We welcome as much peace as is possible.

With harsh and punishing people, we know to apply 1 Corinthians 13. We don't keep record of wrongs, and we don't assume the worst. We know that with God's help, love does not fail. We remember the Lord's words from Matthew 5:43–48.

With demanding and pushy people, we know to remember Colossians 3:22–24 as well as Matthew 11:28–30. Jesus is the best of masters. No one loves us and provides for us like Jesus. We're blessed to wear the name of Christ, to belong to Christ, and to represent Christ. We trust the Lord for relief, reward, and vindication.

Strange Blessings

In everything give thanks, for this is the will of God in Christ Jesus for you.

1 Thessalonians 5:18

Sometimes we get the strangest of blessings. School was closed on a recent rainy holiday, but I was in the office a bit early. It was a combination of being behind and needing to complete a less-than-desirable assignment. I got a text from a fine young student, "Will you be in your office today?" I responded, "I am." He needed a short face-to-face visit. I'm seldom in the right place at the right time. It was a pleasure to be able to offer help without even having to leave my chair.

When we toured the new North Alabama Medical Center in Florence recently, I was blessed to walk in with two precious long-time friends. Just seeing them makes any day better. Once inside, we encountered several other pleasant and encouraging friends—major serendipity.

South African friends needed to live closer to their fine ministry work in the town of Vredenburg. Months of searching had led to no affordable local option. A house came available in nearby Hopefield. As soon as they signed to buy it, a house in Vredenburg—directly across from the church building—went on the market. I know this sounds bad. Where's the blessing? It's really a great story of God's providence. At some degree of risk, Phillip and Roslyn were able to move forward on the Vredenburg house. They put the Hopefield house on the market, and it sold in a single day! We were blessed to see our friends so blessed (Rom 12:15).

We needed more investigation before buying a coffee table at a local antique store. Wanting to be efficient and pay for everything at once, we asked the staff to hold our other small purchases. Among them was a wooden African figure and a way-cool Frankenstein nutcracker. As we looked in an adjacent store, a clerk from the first store came to find us. "I'm so sorry, but another customer has mistakenly taken your bag of items." I hate to lose way-cool things. The next day, we got a happy call. To my surprise, the people who took our bag brought it back. Frankenstein now lives on the table by my side of the bed. He's very happy there.

In virtually any store of any type, whatever catches my eye proves to be the most expensive item. In the same antique store that lost our bag, we found a billy club with character. I'm thinking $20. Turns out, it was way less than $20, and it was on sale. I have no plans to tap anyone, but I like my $3.50 stick.

I awakened way too early on a Sunday morning in the fall. Since it was almost daylight and the leaves needed attention, I got the rake and started. The goal was four to six cans full of leaves. It took only eight cans to get the bulk of them to the pile. The yard looked better, and when my used-to-be muscles stop hurting, that will be yet another strange blessing.

We love and appreciate God's big blessings (John 1:12–16 and 3:16; Rom 5:6–8 and 8:1; 1 Cor 15:50–58; Eph 1:3–14 and 2:4–10). At the same time, we love and appreciate the smaller, unexpected blessings that God sends us every day. They also feed our souls.

Edges

For the word of God is living and powerful, and sharper than any two-edged sword, piercing even to the division of soul and spirit, and joints and marrow, and is a discerner of the thoughts and intents of the heart.

Hebrews 4:12

I have a fascination with edged instruments. Because people know this and are good to me, I have various knives, a sword, a sickle, and two scythes. The sickle is the one with the short handle. The scythes are the two-handed, long-handled tools like the Grim Reaper wields. I know only because I googled it.

For various reasons, several of my edged items have long been left dull. Memories of cuts make that tolerable, but I still prefer all the blades extra-sharp. Reminds me of a man back home in the days of my youth. When we asked him, "How sharp is your knife?" He'd always reply, "Don't get too close, or it will cut your breath off." We always kept our distance.

While the "edge of the sword" stories in Scripture often grab our attention, it's the metaphorical use of that phrase that carries the greater blessing for us today.

On the negative side, the tongue of the temptress proves "sharp as a two-edged sword" (Prov 5:3–6). It's as if a blade with a single edge is insufficient to convey the danger. The illicit conversation is as smooth as oil and drips with honey, but the results are deadly. And we know that this devastating combination isn't limited to one gender. Sharp tongues, whether cutting or beguiling, don't bless on any level.

On the positive side, the metaphor of the two-edged sword turns our minds to Hebrews 4:12. Again, a single edge can't quite say enough. However sharp and piercing we might know or imagine, the power of the living word of the living God is greater. Preachers have long reminded us that God's word cuts going and coming. We sometimes hear that in terms of efficiency and irresistibility. Sometimes, we hear it in in terms of both defeating evil and protecting the saints. In addition, we think of "living" as active, never dormant, and never dull. It's a word that never fails.

As believers, we read Hebrews 4:12 on the positive side of salvation and sanctification. God's word is truth (John 17:17), reveals truth (John 5:36–39), and calls us to love truth (1 Pet 1:22–23; 2 Thess 2:9–12)

The edged imagery continues in the Bible's last book. When John sees "one like the Son of Man," "out of His mouth went a sharp two-edged sword" (Rev 1:16). In the letter to Pergamos, Jesus is described as "He who has the sharp two-edged sword" (Rev 2:12).

We love the richness and the reminder of these words. There's no way and no reason to separate Jesus Christ from the word. He is the Word incarnate (John 1:1–14). Only Jesus perfectly lived God's word (1 Pet 2:22–24). No one ever employed God's word with greater mastery or effect (Luke 2:45–47; Matt 4:1–11; Matt 7:28–29). It's our Lord who masterfully wields the sword of God to our blessing and benefit.

God Is Better than We Know

Oh, taste and see that the Lord is good; blessed is the man who trusts in Him!

Psalm 34:8

At the end of a challenging week, God sent a set of amazing blessings (Jam 1:17). It's not like that's unusual, but these joys were especially timely and welcome.

A personnel decision at work could have been sticky. Both teachers were well-qualified to staff an upcoming course. The new man was willing, but his one caveat was that he not harm or discourage the other teacher. The other teacher chose to welcome a bit of schedule relief and said so in the kindest of ways. As I shared this with a colleague, his response was, "It's amazing what we can accomplish when everyone works for the glory of God." No egos and no competition led to no stress and no worries. And everyone involved felt blessed.

A graduate had long been pursuing recognition as a military chaplain. After years of study, hours of prayer, and a jillion and nine hoops, he emailed word of his victory. The man has a great heart and a boatload of skill. Only God knows how many and how much he will bless. In the spirit of Romans 12:15 and 1 Thessalonians 5:16–18, he completed the trifecta:

- He gave God the glory.
- He shared His joy with us.
- And He expressed glowing, heartfelt thanks.

He thinks we blessed him. We think he blessed us. And within God's grace, we're all right.

On the same afternoon, a major (at least to me) publishing project (this book) took a series of positive turns. I was sent a set of essential inquiries that moved the project forward. These questions asked things that I had not yet even begun to consider. The message these queries sent me was pure Philippians 2:3–4. Good people were looking out for my interests, sacrificing time, and investing talent to help me. God bless them every one!

Finally, another email arrived. A brother obviously had been praying over one of my pressure points. He's as busy as anybody on the planet, but he took time to do some research and type a message that spoke to my need. It's Philippians 2 again, combined with Romans 12:10–13 and 1 Thessalonians 4:9–10. I was receiving high level ministry and being educated in service.

Such blessings deserve to be shared, so I did—verbally and by email. But they deserved to be shared more broadly and more permanently. That's why you're reading about them now.

My challenging week was being challenged and overcome by Galatians 6:9–10. Good people were doing good to me—more good than they may have realized. Their kindness led to Proverbs 25:11, 25, the power of both "a word fitly spoken" and "good news from a far country."

What's one to do in the face of such blessings? You already know.

- Give God the glory.

- Share the joy and encouragement with others. Apply Philippians 4:9 and 1 Corinthians 11:1 by imitating the worthy examples of these ministers of grace.

- And continue to express glowing, heartfelt thanks. We don't forget those who love us.

How Did I Miss That?

Seeing many things, but you do not observe; opening the ears, but he does not hear.

Isaiah 42:20

My technically antique truck has a warning tone that reminds me when I leave the lights on. I've learned that the warning now works part-time. Bless her heart, a neighbor recently rang the doorbell to tell me the lights were on. A few nights later, I left them on again and completely depleted the battery. It took jumper cables and a battery charger to get going again.

How could a semi-functional adult walk around his own vehicle in the dark and fail to notice that the lights were left on? Should I plead the fifth? Chalk it up to fatigue? Say that these things just happen? Claim to have a lot on my mind? Argue diminished capacity? There are better options.

- *Humility.* What else do I look at without seeing? Am I missing obvious opportunities to serve and to teach? Am I missing obvious warnings that God is sending?

- *Gratitude.* The warning tone still works sometimes. Sometimes I notice the lights left on. Our neighbor chose to help us. And I don't always fail to see my errors.

- *The opportunity to form a needed new habit.* Always check the lights. Don't depend on the ding-ding-ding. Get off autopilot and attend to reality at an improved level.

- *Reflection.* Apply "how did I miss that" spiritually. Think of Scripture and be taught by God. That's a HUGE opportunity.

As God commissioned Isaiah, He told the prophet to warn the people, "Keep on hearing, but do not understand; keep on seeing, but do not perceive" (Isa 6:9–10). That wasn't God's will for them, but He knew their hearts. Sadly, the nation fell because a stunning majority would not see the obvious or hear God's truth.

Isaiah 6:9–10 was quoted by Jesus as He answered the excellent question, "Why do You speak to them in parables?" (Matt 13:10ff). "I speak to them in parables because seeing they do not see, and hearing they do not hear, nor do they understand." What a fearsome thought! God is willing to withhold His truth from those who choose to reject it. In grace, He "hides" His word in plain sight. It's there, only microns away, if they'll just open their eyes, ears, and hearts.

Isaiah 6:9–10 was quoted by Paul to Jewish leaders in Rome who chose to disbelieve his teaching of the gospel, even though he taught "from both the Law of Moses and the Prophets, from morning till evening" (Acts 28:23ff). He accurately connected Jesus to their history and their Scripture. None are so blind as those who will not see; none are so deaf as those who refuse to hear. Without willingness to see and hear, the gospel was rejected. It could neither save nor heal.

Both inattention and willful closure of eyes and ears aren't limited to one group or one era. Both can afflict any of us anywhere anytime. And these afflictions always rob us of God's blessings.

Out of Date

The entirety of Your word is truth, and every one of Your righteous judgments endures forever.

Psalm 119:160

Please don't read this as a medical recommendation, but I don't care about the expiration or "best by" date on my food. If it looks okay and passes the smell test, I'll eat it. To the best of my knowledge, that has done me no harm thus far.

I'm both amused and amazed that some of my friends think so differently. Any food that's considered out of date gets tossed immediately. My friends don't understand what they sometimes see as my depression-era mentality. And I don't understand them tossing perfectly good food. On a happy note, we've adopted a live and let live approach to this minor difference of opinion. A few of them even give me their out-of-date items, which I happily consume.

I keep learning that I'm out-of-date—archaic, anachronistic, and behind the times—in many ways.

- I have an electric blower, but still rake my leaves. Sometimes it's for exercise, and sometimes it's sublimation. Either way, the leaves get moved. I even have a spare rake in case the current one breaks.

- I still scrub the siding on the house rather than paying someone to power wash it. I need to do the occasional job where progress is visible and immediate. It blesses me.

- Same deal with washing the car and my old truck by hand. I'm old, and I have never run a vehicle through a car wash. It's a record I hope to maintain.

I love the fact that some things never go out of date—they're both precious and timeless.

- Beautiful sunrises and sunsets. Rainbows. The first fall colors. The first green of spring. All fit Psalm 19 for as long as the earth stands.

- Beautiful singing, especially psalms, hymns, and spiritual songs (Col 3:16).

- Beautiful children. Their laughter. Their energy. Their optimism. Their potential (Luke 2:52).

- Beautiful souls of any age. People who embrace life, bless others, and love God (Luke 2:25–38).

- Trust in God and God's word (Prov 3:5–6; Job 13:15).

- Kindness. Courtesy. Treating people like they matter (Gen 2:26–27; Rom 12:9–13; Phil 2:3–4).

- Gratitude. Appreciation. Thankfulness (1 Thess 5:18; 1 Tim 2:1–2).

- Love for God and love for people (Matt 22:34–40; John 13:34–35; 1 John 4).

Standing in Line for Visitation

Therefore, my beloved, as you have always obeyed, not as in my presence only, but now much more in my absence, work out your own salvation with fear and trembling; for it is God who works in you both to will and to do for His good pleasure.

Philippians 2:12–13

The son of a long-time friend had died. He was two years my junior. Visitation with the family involved a rather long line in a nearby church building. That's where the story starts.

I was in line between two precious Christians and a local public official. I couldn't have picked a better spot. I learned family news, church news, legal news, medical news, economic news, and more—without any tuition or fees.

Conversation never ran dry, but every time it tried, someone stepped over to speak to one of us. Saw people I'd not seen in years, met new people, and was invited to pray for people. It became a mini-ministry clinic.

The day before, a gathering celebrating the well-lived life of a neighbor was providentially similar. Saw people I needed to see and heard things I needed to hear. They opened the floor to the audience and got away with it. They even sang "Over the Rainbow." It blessed my heart.

I'm reminded that God can bless anyone, anywhere, at any time. And He does this so often. There's the odd story of Abraham meeting Melchizedek, king of Salem and priest of God Most High, following the first rescue of Lot (Gen 14:18ff). Is this just a set up for Hebrews 5 and 7? Or is it a reminder that we never know when we'll meet a fellow servant and have opportunity to be a blessing?

There's the way cool story of Abraham's oldest and most trusted servant finding Isaac's wife-to-be Rebekah through her respectful and generous service (Gen 24:10ff). It's a story bathed in prayer, with a bit of mystery, a nice surprise, and a happy ending.

There's the story of Moses finding a new home, a new job, and a wife because he chose to go the second mile in helping an unknown group of women (Exod 2:16ff). No miracle, sign, or wonder—just good people doing good things and opening the door for God's blessings.

Like Zacchaeus, sometimes all we need to do to invite God's blessing is to be present and awake (Luke 19). Admittedly, Zacchaeus did much more, but that's another category of blessing. God let the chief tax collector participate in his redemption just like He lets us (Phil 2:12–13).

As a simple person, I draw the simplest of conclusions:

- Be where you ought to be. The house of sorrow is often that place (Eccles 7:1–4).

- God can make virtually anywhere the place we ought to be (John 4; Phlm 10–11).

- Whatever good we can do in any moment, do it (Acts 3:1–10; Luke 10:25–37).

- Ally with good people. Help them. And don't get in their way (Luke 9:49–50).

- Never miss a chance to serve, bless, or protect (Matt 7:12, 20:24–28).

God never stops teaching if we are willing to learn. God never stops blessing if we are willing to be grateful and pay it forward in His name. God never stops helping us grow if we keep loving Him.

Leaf Lessons

For he shall be like a tree planted by the waters, which spreads out its roots by the river, and will not fear when heat comes; but its leaf will be green, and will not be anxious in the year of drought, nor will cease from yielding fruit.

Jeremiah 17:8

The biggest tree at our house was damaged by lightning several years back. People stopped by, wanting to give us a price for removing it. "You know it's dead," was the lead sentence in each brief conversation. I didn't and neither did the tree. It bears a major scar but continues to flourish. This year it produced what seems to be a record number of leaves.

I like the tree and its scar. Things made by God are more resilient than things made by humans. Having a scar doesn't make a tree—or a person—worthless or unable. Both trees and people can survive far more and far worse than we realize.

As an oak, our scarred but vibrant tree is deciduous; it loses its leaves every fall. Still, it makes me think of the description of the righteous in Psalm 1:3, "He shall be like a tree planted by the rivers of water, that brings forth its fruit in its season, whose leaf does not wither, and whatever he does shall prosper." While the acorns aren't fruit to me, the squirrels seem to love them.

Besides the three big trees near the street, our lot is tree-lined at the rear. In summer, we love the shade and the deep green colors. In the fall, we deal with a jillion falling leaves—every one of them some shade of brown. I don't mind that, as it gives me pause to reflect.

- On a quiet morning, you can hear the leaves fall. It almost sounds like rain. I've never been sure why it's such a soothing sound.

- There are too many leaves to mulch effectively. Raking and transporting them to the end of the street provide an abundance of needed exercise. Until the next batch falls, you can see and enjoy your progress (Eccles 2:24 and 3:22).

- As the next batch falls, we're reminded of how much we don't control. They don't fall on command, and they don't stay on demand. They follow a cycle that we didn't choose, and we can't control. And there's no need to fuss or stress about it (Matt 6:34).

- Neighbors think it strange that I sometimes rake leaves before daylight. The leaves don't seem to mind. It's convenient for me, there are no distractions, and generally the wind stays calm. Plus, it's good to enjoy the occasional harmless odd behavior.

- As I age, my used-to-be muscles remind me that I won't be raking my own leaves forever. There was a time when I could have raked the entire lawn in a single long day. That time has long passed. Its passing reminds me of Psalm 90:10 and Ecclesiastes 12:1–5. Some of the trees that produce those leaves will likely be here long after I am gone.

- Dealing with the leaves reminds me of the power of perseverance. No matter how little I get done today, I'll eventually complete the job if I don't quit. Quitting isn't a viable option. Reminds me of Galatians 6:9.

- When I pile the leaves instead of letting them blow over and plague our neighbors, I'm reminded of Galatians 6:10 and Matthew 7:12. Maybe I need more leaf lessons.

The Coolest Things

*For we have great joy and consolation in your love, because
the hearts of the saints have been refreshed by you, brother.*

Philemon 7

The food is consistent and cheap, so Laura and I were eating at a local Taco Bell. A ball of energy burst through the door with the exclamation, "My teacher! Momma, you have to meet my teacher!"

I was unsurprised with mom's two questions: "How are we doing?" and "You're not seeing problems with ADHD, are you?" Laura assured mom that daughter was doing well and properly deflected the second question. It was fun to see the kid so happy.

That was our second such episode in recent days. Though I have no business in a pizza place, we visit Cicis every couple of months. I tell myself that the salad helps balance the carbs. As we were leaving, a little guy ran up yelling, "Mrs. Bagents!" as he hugged Laura. He, also, introduced her to his mom.

These days, teaching seems more challenging than ever. I have no illusion that teachers choose their profession for the paycheck. The stress, demands, and challenges wouldn't allow a mere monetary selection. But the opportunity to make a positive difference in the life of a child, that's priceless.

Of course, you don't have to be employed as a teacher to make such a difference. Think of families who do foster care and families who have adopted. Think of grandparents who have reared their grandchildren. And that is nothing short of wonderful.

Think of the Bible's positive message for those who bless children: "Then little children were brought to Him that He might put His hands on them and pray, but the disciples rebuked them. But Jesus said, 'Let the little children come to Me, and do not forbid them, for of such is the kingdom of heaven'" (Matt 19:13–14).

It's not difficult to see the implications:

- If the Lord of heaven and earth had time for children, surely His disciples must.

- The opportunity to bless a child is itself a blessing.

- A person too busy to bless a child has priority problems—and heart problems, too.

- Even the oldest of us can keep learning from "the mouths (and actions) of babes."

- A person being protected from contact with children is being tragically over-protected.

There's another set of lessons from Laura's recent positive encounters. Both helped my heart as well as hers. We know that truth from Romans 12:15: "Rejoice with those who rejoice." We see it in Romans 13:7: "Render therefore to all their due ... honor to whom honor." It's the principle we read in Proverbs 31:31 as well. There's joy in seeing those we love appreciated for their good hearts and good works. And in Christ, we get to be known for loving the whole family of God (John 13:34–35; 1 John 4:7–21).

Surprises

The righteous will answer Him, saying, "Lord, when did we see You hungry and feed You, or thirsty and give You drink? When did we see You a stranger and take You in, or naked and clothe You? Or when did we see You sick, or in prison, and come to You?" And the King will answer and say to them, "Assuredly, I say to you, inasmuch as you did it to one of the least of these My brethren, you did it to Me."

Matthew 25:37–40

Recently, one of my brothers and his wife came to Florence for a work-related conference. They kindly chose to visit our Wednesday evening worship, planning to surprise us. Turns out that I was speaking in Tuscumbia that evening. The eighteenth-century Scottish poet Robert Burns nailed it about the best laid plans of mice and men. Sometimes we're the "surpriser," and sometimes we're the "surprisee."

After our Wednesday night miss, we scheduled dinner together for Friday night. We followed the fine dinner and good visit with a walk through a Florence downtown event—First Fridays. We were surprised to meet several friends during the walk. As we were almost done, up came a couple we're planning a South African mission trip with. There was no way for them to know that the bulk of our dinner conversation centered around the mission trip to Cape Town. And now our guests got to meet the rest of that mission team.

One day I took a bunch of bargain books to the checkout counter at a local store. The clerk asked, "Aren't these the ones that are twenty cents each?" I surprised myself by saying, "Sorry, I don't have a clue." (That should not have been surprising as it is often true). That day, all my books were twenty cents each. What a nice surprise! The retail price on one of them was $78.

I surprised myself three times one week. I found a set of notes I really needed. It didn't even take long to find them. Twice, I googled a matter of interest and found even more information than was anticipated. That NEVER (almost never) happens.

On the flip side, I googled a local thrift store to see the hours of operation. The store has a website, and the website said, "Open now, open until 3:00." The website was wrong. Not only was the store closed, but it was the day of the Handy Parade. Parades and I don't get along. Bad surprise times two.

You already known that biblical surprises are a mixed bag. That's easily seen in Matthew 25. When Jesus praises the righteous, their response is sweet surprise, "Lord, when did we see You hungry and feed You, or thirsty and give You drink? When did we see You a stranger and take You in, or naked and clothe You? Or when did we see You sick or in prison and come to You?" It's as if they never thought of their service to God's people as direct service to God.

On the other hand, the condemned are equally surprised. Read Matthew 25:41–46. They can't believe their neglect of the hungry, thirsty, strangers, sick, and needy was neglect of Jesus. They are just as surprised as the condemned from Matthew 7:21-23. They are shocked to learn that God doesn't see or judge like humans do (1 Sam 16:7; Isa 55:8–9; John 7:24).

We see the same lesson in Revelation 2–3. The impoverished Christians in Smyrna got the joy of being called rich by Jesus (2:9). The complacent in Sardis had "a name that you are alive," but Jesus declared them dead (3:1–2). The prideful in Laodicea viewed themselves as rich and in need of nothing, but Jesus deemed them "wretched, miserable, poor, blind, and naked" (3:17). What a set of surprises! How we need to hear and heed the wisdom of Jesus (Rev 3:22).

Playing With Names

If anyone speaks, let him speak as the oracles of God.

1 Peter 4:11

Some of us like playing with names.

- Hobby Lobby becomes Hob Lob, Hub Lub, Hubby Lubby, or on a different level, the China Store (just look at the stickers).

- Wal-Mart is sometimes Wally World and sometimes Waldo's.

- We've been known to call Interstate 65 the Great Alabama Racetrack and Parking Lot. That's not an efficient renaming, but it is highly accurate.

As much as I like playing with names, sometimes I don't like the "name play" practiced by others. How does a bank expect customer loyalty when it changes names every few months? Some of the nursing homes in our area have changed names enough times that some can't remember what's current and correct and others stopped caring. I respect the changes to Mumbai and Kolkata, but I still miss hearing Bombay and Calcutta. Do you remember when Prince temporarily changed his name to some set of symbols that had no pronunciation? I laughed every time the media described him as "the artist formerly known as Prince."

Some names and titles shouldn't be played with.

- I so regret that "Oh my God!" has become such a trite and obnoxious byline (Exod 20:7).

- I so regret that so many religious leaders wear the title "reverend." Look it up—it still means holy, awe inspiring, terrible. It asserts a clergy/laity distinction that's foreign to the Bible (1 Pet 2:9–10; 1 Sam 2:2; Mark 10:17–18).

- I so regret when "preacher" is thought of as lazy, self-righteous, and judgmental. I hope I always feel a strong obligation to assist that concept into extinction (John 7:24; Rom 14).

- I so regret that the phrase "do-gooder" has become an insult and an accusation. We want to be people who do good. Jesus went about doing good (Acts 10:38). I admire those who do good and those who expect the best of others (Titus 2:14, 3:1, 8, and 14).

- I regret that even endearing terms like brother and sister are often misused as titles. Those words should carry the weight of love and affection. We're so blessed to be family in Christ (Gal 3:26–27; John 1:11–13).

There are times and situations when it's fun to play with certain words. And there is never a time or situation to play fast and loose with God's word.

Ain't Nothing Folks Won't Do

In those days there was no king in Israel; everyone did what was right in his own eyes.

Judges 21:25

"There ain't nothing folks won't do." I think this is my dad's favorite statement of wisdom. He knows the grammar is challenged, but he's been around long enough to recognize and face reality. This sad truth fits so many situations that make national headlines:

- A teacher "runs away with" an underage student.

- A homicidal bomber kills himself while blowing up a school or a church building.

- A leader resigns in disgrace for maleficence but declares himself to be moving into a new phase of service.

- A parent kills his or her own child for being inconvenient.

- A husband and father leaves his family of twenty-plus years because he has found his "soulmate."

- An athlete unethically takes money from his college and celebrates when "they" get caught.

- A burglar sues his victim because he was injured while committing the crime.

Such stories amaze me. Perhaps I should be more amazed when I realize that I'm "folks" too.

- Why am I still tempted to make excuses for my sins when there's not a single biblical example of such making a difference with God?

- Why am I still tempted to think that I'm qualified to judge the motives of others?

- Why am I still tempted to love things too much and people too little?

- Why am I still impatient when God has been so patient with me?

- Why do I still sometimes fail to pray?

- Why do I still battle the illusion that I can make others do what I want them to do?

- Why am I still tempted to stress, push, and hurry instead of doing right and leaving outcomes to God?

Biblical solutions abound. We can trust God with all our hearts (Prov 3:5). We can fear God and keep His commandments (Eccles 12:13). We can be guided by love above all things (Matt 22:36–40; 1 Pet 4:8). We can be very careful about overestimating ourselves (1 Cor 10:12). We can pray for wisdom (Jam 1:5). We can cast all our care on Him (1 Pet 5:7). And we can continually seek God's forgiveness (Luke 18:13).

True Beauty

Do not let your adornment be merely outward—arranging the hair, wearing gold, or putting on fine apparel—rather let it be the hidden person of the heart, with the incorruptible beauty of a gentle and quiet spirit, which is very precious in the sight of God.

1 Peter 3:3–4

I still enjoy the Robert Palmer lyrics, "A pretty face don't make no pretty heart." Bad grammar aside, they express truth: looks can be deceiving. The words of Jesus from John 7:24 come to mind: "Do not judge according to appearance, but judge with righteous judgment."

To use the common metaphor, we know that we can't always judge a book by its cover. Within academia, many expensive and valuable books come in traditional drab colors with no artwork and no curb appeal.

"A pretty face don't make no pretty heart," but neither does a pretty face indicate deceit, selfishness, or treachery. We all know physically beautiful people who are just as beautiful morally and spiritually.

On the flip side, being plain in appearance says nothing about one's heart either. We remember the famous description of the Messiah from Isaiah 53:2, "He has no form or comeliness, and when we see Him, there is no beauty that we should desire Him." As we read the gospels, it's clear that people couldn't discern the divine character of Jesus merely through His physical appearance.

"A pretty face don't make no pretty heart," but it's been my experience that a good heart and the good actions that flow from it often enhance a person's appearance. I'd never do rating scales or claim expertise, but I know that people with beautiful souls look good to me. It warms my heart to see them, whether young and vibrant or weathered and worn.

Maybe we're wise to consider accompanying statements about beauty. For example, "Beauty is in the eye of the beholder." While there may be commonalities in what most people consider beautiful, there's also a world of variation.

To whatever degree that beauty is in the eye of the beholder, do we realize that we can choose what we consider to be beautiful? Of course, I'm thinking far more about attributes and attitudes than about physical features. When we choose to find love, joy, peace, and the remaining fruit of the Spirit beautiful, we are choosing to agree with God. And we make it far easier to imitate and internalize those virtues. We're blessed to appreciate all the beauty of God's creation, but no other beauty compares to the beauty of holiness—the beauty of God Himself.

Morning Started Off "Quite"

Sing praise to the Lord, you saints of His and give thanks to the remembrance of His holy name, for His anger is but for a moment, his favor is for life; weeping may endure for a night, but joy comes in the morning.

Psalm 30:4–5

A friend once sent me the following: "The morning has started off quite." I assume it's a typo, and the intended word was "quiet." In case I'm wrong, let's consider it a fill-in-the-blank: "The morning has started off quite _____." Choices include well, badly, interestingly, lazily, ironically, painfully, happily, hopeful, noisily, prayerfully, slowly, rapidly, Monday-ish, blessed, quietly, tragically, confusingly, impressively, disappointingly, uneventfully, strangely, reflectively, mournfully, predictably, productively, and normally. Perhaps I should have stopped sooner. The possibilities seem infinite.

So far, I'm resisting the temptation to alphabetize my list. I could never choose "normally" because I don't think I know what normal might look like. Many weeks have multiple Monday mornings. "Painfully" is so imprecise—is it take-a-pill painful or a deep hurting of the heart? Both "slowly" and "rapidly" can be either a blessing or a curse depending on the situation.

Other words on our list are stunningly fluid. "Strangely" would vary from person to person. I don't find it strange to have people waiting at the office door, one to thank me and another to scold. "Impressively" depends on what we choose to be impressed by. On a recent challenging morning, a friend sent me John 16:33 by email. It had just the effect she hoped it would.

Speaking of fluidity, any version of "It's been quite a morning," is wonderfully flexible. It ranks right up there with "How about that?", "He's something," and "What do you know?" Sometimes we're quite wise not to pin ourselves down. There are lines that help us avoid complaining without being dishonest.

The best words on our list are wonderfully under our direct control. Every morning can begin prayerfully (Mark 1:35; 1 Thess 5:17; 1 Tim 2:1–4). Every morning can be blessed and hopeful if we have the faith to see God's hand (Lam 3:22–24). The Bible even offers ways that we can invite more of God's blessings (Mal 3:10; Luke 6:38; Jam 1:5–6). Every morning can begin with heartfelt reflection on the goodness of God (Psa 136, 138, and 139). We can also reflect on our spiritual condition, either to rejoice in hope or make essential corrections (2 Cor. 13:5; Gal 6:1–5). We can reflect on the needs of others (Phil. 2:3–4)

Some of the words on our list merit contemplation. If my morning started disappointingly, in what sense and for what reasons? If I'm disappointed in God, I need to adjust my thinking: God always does right. If I'm disappointed in myself, could I have done better, or did I imagine more control than I had? If I'm disappointed in others, am I being fair and gracious, or were my expectations unrealistic? Even if I'm disappointed, how can I learn, grow, and do better?

Every new morning is a gift from God (Acts 17:28). With His help, we can put a fine word in the blank of "The morning started off quite _____." The Lord can rescue even the oddest and most difficult of mornings (John 20:1–18). He does that for us more often than we know.

Junk and Treasures

But what things were gain to me, these I have counted loss for Christ. Yet indeed I also count all things loss for the excellence of the knowledge of Christ Jesus my Lord, for whom I have suffered the loss of all things, and count them as rubbish, that I may gain Christ.

Philippians 3:7–8

We were in a thrift shop recently when a friend asked, "What is it that makes us want to look through other people's junk?" Good question, for which I don't know the definitive answer. Could it be that we love bargains that much? Could it be that we believe that somewhere among the junk there's a treasure to be captured? For me on that day, it was predominately the opportunity to capture a few more books for the Overton Memorial Library.

I see much truth in the adage, "One man's trash is another man's treasure." Preferences, needs, whims, memories, and idiosyncrasies can help us value the strangest of things. To date, I'm still ambulatory without a cane, but I love canes. The last one I bought is acrylic with a handle that only works in the right hand. It was just too cool to pass up. The elephant head carving I saw recently in a thrift store almost demanded that I bring it home. It was unique, wooden, and priced to sell. Some things we buy just so we can give them away. We don't think an inexpensive gift carries any insult at all. We'd never check on the price of a gift that we received.

I know I need to be careful with the "junk" that I buy. Even the most precious items are temporal—destructible, "stealable," and ultimately of little consequence. All such items may wind up in a series of yard sales one day. While fun to look at, such items should never define who we are. They should never have too big a place in our hearts.

On the other hand, there are imperishable, permanent, and rich treasures that God keeps recommending to us. You are welcome to add to the list:

- There are good deeds done quietly for others (Matt 6:1–4).

- There are prayers that rise before the throne of God (Matt 6:5–15).

- There are quiet sacrifices made to honor God and to remind ourselves that He is Lord (Matt 6:16–18).

Isn't it fascinating that Matthew 6:19–21 urges us to lay up the right treasures in the right location? And the text makes no bones about it: these are treasures that we lay up for ourselves. We're told that twice for emphasis.

The things we choose to treasure say much about our hearts. The location of our treasures says even more: "For where your treasure is, there your heart will be also" (Matt 6:21). I like the thought of there being no junk and no clutter in heaven. I love the thought of the treasures we send ahead bringing everlasting glory to God. What better treasure than a soul won to Christ through the power of the gospel? What sweeter treasure than a person precious to God being treated as precious just because God wills it to be so (Gen 1:26–27; John 3:16, 13:34–35; Rom 12:9–21; Gal 6:10)?

Bad grammar, but accurate theology: "God don't make no junk." Whenever we have opportunity to encourage a soul toward heaven, even that opportunity is a treasure to be seized. God can take the little that we're able to do and multiply it immeasurably. And as He does that, He continues to claim us among His precious treasures.

Math Problems

Trust in the Lord with all your heart, and lean not on your own understanding; in all your ways acknowledge Him, and He shall direct your paths.

Proverbs 3:5–6

On a recent stop at a burger place, the register showed the cashier that she owed us $.40 in change. She removed three coins and then asked her manager, "Is this 40 cents?" Turns out that it was, but if I were the manager, she'd never work the register again. My confidence in her would never recover.

We bought some used books for the school library. Total was $16.50. The register had no ones, but there was a five-dollar bill. I told the nice clerk, "I think I can make change. How about I give you another $1.50 and you give me $5.00?" She "locked up" immediately. After an awkward pause and a nod of approval from a fellow worker, she handed me the $5.00, but I could tell that she still wasn't comfortable. "How about you check our math while I box my books?" I asked. She checked the math twice with paper and pen. As I headed away, she said, "Thank you for your donation." I was still stuck on $21.50 minus $16.50 equals $5.00, but we parted on friendly terms.

Math isn't everyone's strong suit. I have days when it isn't mine. Isn't the human brain amazing? It can run a multifunctional, complex system (our bodies), and then balk at elementary calculations. It can help you make a great choice on the purchase of a car and then fail to remember where you parked the thing. It can reproduce the sweetest ancient memory, complete with sounds and smells, and then let you call a dear old friend by the wrong name.

I love the ancient quotation from Greek philosopher Heraclitus: "Much learning does not teach understanding." While we're grateful to be "fearfully and wonderfully made" (Psalm 139), we dare not "think more highly of self than [we] ought to think (Rom 12:3). We dare not rely more on ourselves than we do on the Lord (Prov 16:25; Jer 10:23). We're wise to stay coachable (Prov 15:22) and correctable (Prov 17:10).

On a trip to Huntsville, Alabama, I knew how to get from one bookstore to the next, but Laura's GPS begged to differ. I just needed to make a left on Holmes Avenue, but the GPS wanted two extra turns. In a moment of weakness I decided to listen to Laura. Turns out that there's a bridge out on Holmes Avenue and two additional turns were essential. It's not exactly math, but it's good for me to recognize my limitations and to be reminded that there are better sources of information than my own thinking.

I once bought almost 50 items that were priced at $4.00 each. Laura sent me with enough money to make the nearly $200 purchase. At checkout, the manager said, "That will be $50." I responded, "Would you like to check your math?" She responded, "That will be $50." I responded, "You know I'm not allowed to steal from you." She responded, "That will be $50." I'm slow, but sometimes I eventually understand. She had the authority to reduce the price, she chose to reduce the price, and my job was to pay up and say thank you. That wasn't a math problem; it was a grace problem. She was offering great kindness, and I was missing her point.

Aren't you glad that God loves us limitations and all? Aren't you glad that God extends grace to us and lets us extend kindness to one another? I know I am.

Adventures

Therefore, as we have opportunity, let us do good to all, especially to those who are of the household of faith.

Galatians 6:10

W e like simple, positive, and inexpensive adventures. Sometimes those come in the most unexpected ways. As we paid for some books at the Homewood Public Library, we asked the nice clerk to recommend a place for lunch. She suggested a short drive to downtown where there would be numerous options. As we approached the area, there was a single parking space open just across from Johnny's. We happily claimed it. There wasn't even a meter.

The library employee had described Johnny's as "a meat and three." It was that and more, with great food within our price range. Nice people, nice atmosphere—it was the kind of place that makes you want to come back again.

The older I get, the more I like nice. Specifically, I like people who are nice to me. On the other hand, I'm trying to pay more attention to being nice to others. Besides being one aspect of love and decency (think John 13:34–35; 1 Cor 13; Phil 2:1–4), it's highly functional even from an earthly point of view. Most people tend to be reciprocal—they treat you about like you treat them. If you're pleasant and engaging, they tend to follow suit.

In our everyday interactions with others, we become part of their adventures. A pleasant look, a warm greeting, or an act of kindness warms their hearts and invites them to treat others with kindness and respect. The opposite is also true. Our coolness or neglect could tilt things toward the negative. We have more power and influence than we sometimes think.

In that God gives us power, influence, and opportunity, we get to use those to His glory (Gal 6:10). The nice woman in the library could have brushed off my question. Why take a risk on helping a stranger? Who knows if he'll even listen? If he listens, takes my advice, and things go wrong, will he blame me? Who needs the hassle?

On the positive side, the questions work much better. Why not help a stranger? Hebrews 13:1–2 comes to mind. If he listens, maybe I've made a friend. At the very least, I've practiced my communication skills. Better to try than not to try. If he listens, takes the advice, and things go well, maybe he will imitate the example and "pay it forward" to bless others. Why waste an opportunity to do good?

As Christians, we're always on the clock—24/7/365. We continuously represent Christ to the world—and to one another. Our mutual adventures are seldom planned, scheduled, or formal. From our limited perspectives, they seem to be happenstance. I don't think they look that way to God. How blessed we'd be to share His viewpoint. Here's an encounter with a soul loved by God. How can I help this person see Jesus? How can I help this person know that God loves him? How can I point this soul toward heaven?

You know what I'm advocating. I'm asking us to make our adventures more purposeful, more spiritual. We know that God works in mysterious ways. Many of those ways may be more "ordinary" and subtle than we would ever imagine.

Much Ado About Nothing

Therefore do not worry about tomorrow, for tomorrow will worry about its own things. Sufficient for the day is its own trouble.

Matthew 6:34

We recently had dramatic predictions of major snow. The National Weather Service issued a winter storm warning. The television stations played up the threat. A few churches cancelled services before a single snowflake fell. Scores followed suit as snow began to fall overnight. More than 200 churches in Alabama cancelled services.

And we awakened Sunday morning to clear roads and a pretty blanket of snow on the grass. By noon, virtually all had melted. It was another case of much ado about ALMOST nothing. That Sunday turned out to be a brisk but beautiful day.

Despite radar, satellites, and computer models, the practical impact of the snow was greatly exaggerated. It leaves many of us feeling like the experts cried wolf. It leaves many of us wondering how much stock to put in future predictions.

It's a striking reminder of how little we know, even about the immediate future. It shouldn't surprise us. From the weather forecast to the dramatic decline of the stock market to the price of gasoline, we don't know what's next. Not only that, we don't even guess well.

What should our limitations teach us? How can our limited knowledge and understanding bless us?

- They remind us that we're not God, and we never will be. God knows all, including us (Psa 139:1–6). We don't even do very well at knowing ourselves.

- They remind us that trusting in people, even the best and most educated people, has major limits (Prov 3:5–

6). Only God is fully trustworthy in all things at all times.

- They remind us that we never know what a day brings (Jam 4:13–17). God always knows what every day brings.

- They remind us that people often over-react to what could happen. To make it worse, we often under-react to what is happening. Without God, we lack balance, perspective, and stability.

- They remind us that good intentions are NOT a safe guide (Acts 23:1). There's no reason to impugn the motives of those who saw the storm as a significant threat. But good motives didn't keep them from over-estimating the storm's impact.

I'm glad that we missed bad weather. I'm glad we enjoyed the beauty of the snow. But I hope we don't miss the lessons. God is always teaching. We need to learn.

Beacons

Let your light so shine before men that they may see your good works and glorify your Father in heaven.

Matthew 5:16

While reading an article, one phrase caught my eye. The author noted that every Christian has the "opportunity to be a beacon of sanity" in this often chaotic and irrational world. As beacons of sanity, we reason and act from a godly perspective, thereby inviting others to see the joy, beauty, wisdom, and power of living God's way (Prov 1:7; Psa 1; John 14:5–6).

As I continued to read that good article, I began to ask myself, "In what other ways can Christians be beacons in this ever-darkening world?" You might enjoy adding to the list below.

- *We can be beacons of hope.* "This hope we have as an anchor of the soul, both sure and steadfast" (Heb 6:19). There is no hope as great as the hope that God has set before us, the hope of everlasting life in His presence!

- *We can be beacons of joy.* Even in the hardest of circumstances, we can choose the joy of serving our God. That's just what Jesus did (Heb 12:1–2). That's just what Paul did (Phil 4:4–9).

- *We can be beacons of peace.* We seek peace, pursue peace, pray for peace, and sacrifice for the sake of peace (John 14:27; Rom 12:9–21; Phil 4:4–9).

- *We can be beacons of truth.* We love the truth, believe the truth, live the truth, and teach the truth (1 Pet 4:11; 3 John 4; John 8:32).

- *We can be beacons of kindness.* We choose kindness, even in the face of cruelty, because that's exactly what our Lord chose (2 Tim 2:24–26; Gal 5:22–23).

- *We can be beacons of responsibility.* We embrace responsibility. We welcome the honor of serving and leading to the glory of God. We love doing good to God's glory (Phil 2:12–13; Eph 2:10; Col 3:23–24; 1 Tim 4:12–16; Titus 2:14, 3:1, 8, and 14).

- *We can be beacons of purity and holiness.* We choose to stand out as "children of God without fault in the midst of a crooked and perverse generation, among whom you shine as lights in the world" (Phil 2:14–16). It is God who makes us shine!

Neurodiversity

Let your speech always be with grace, seasoned with salt, that you may know how you ought to answer each one.

Colossians 4:6

It struck me as funny at first sight. The online advertisement invited me to a webinar that would teach me how to meet the learning needs of "today's neurodiverse students." So many questions:

- In that no two people think and process exactly alike, isn't every individual neurodiverse (cognitively and neurologically unique)? Doesn't it seem foolish to think that any two people always learn in exactly the same ways?

- If our assertion of individual uniqueness is accurate, does this lead to a recommendation of individualized instruction? I love both the idea and the practice of respecting each person, but I know I'm not smart enough to craft and execute an individual learning plan for each student whom I teach. I've never encountered a teacher who was able to do so.

- If our assertion of individual uniqueness is accurate, has that just started? That seems stunningly unlikely. I'd argue that students (humans) have always been neurodiverse.

What does this have to do with God, Scripture, and spiritual growth? Bunches.

For centuries, Bible teachers have reminded us of the diversity of teaching styles and methods within Scripture. We find the nuanced, complex, engaging, repetitive, and well-crafted Old Testament narratives. Think of the Joseph saga in Genesis or the story of David from the books of Samuel. We find the well-ordered and detailed rules of Leviticus and Deuteronomy. We find the poetry—not rhyming, but emotive, creative, and powerful poetic language—of the Psalms.   Figurative speech abounds, stretching our minds. We find the pithy statements and stunning contrasts of Proverbs. We find the challenging, enigmatic, and almost inexplicable paradox within Ecclesiastes.

We find numbers and lists for those whose brains are so constructed. We find emphasis on multi-modal learning by reading, hearing, seeing, doing, and teaching (Phil 4:9). We find history, cultural explanations, geographical guides, and travelogues. We find the cosmic scope and otherworldliness of the apocalyptic sections amazing. It pulls back the mental curtain and makes us contemplate realities we never imagined. And what do we say of the word pictures and heart pictures that Jesus paints in His parables? They grab us by the soul and won't let go.

As we think of these and more, it's as if God knew from before the beginning that His creatures would be neurodiverse. It's as if God planned to offer maximum depth, range and diversity of instruction. It's as if, once again, truths we're emphasizing as cutting edge, God has recognized and engaged from the time of our origin.

Does Scripture direct evidence of God's diverse, inclusive teaching plan? Think of the twin "opposite" truths of Proverbs 26:4–5. Think of that rich phrase "that you may know how to answer each one" from Colossians 4:6. It does not imply a one-means-fits-all approach to teaching. Hebrews 5:12–14 acknowledges levels of knowledge acquisition. John 16:12 reminds us that we sometimes must grow and wait before we learn the fuller truth. And only the Lord knows what we're missing as we marvel at His knowledge of us and our needs.

Growth Orientation

And He Himself gave some to be apostles, some prophets, some evangelists, and some pastors and teachers, for the equipping of the saints for the work of ministry, for the edifying of the body of Christ, till we all come to the unity of the faith and of the knowledge of the Son of God, to a perfect man, to the measure of the stature of the fullness of Christ.

Ephesians 4:11–13

Blessings abound when we choose a growth orientation (mindset, attitude, approach) toward life. By definition, choosing a growth orientation reminds us that we can choose our perspective. The opposite of a growth orientation has been labeled as fixed, stuck, and static. It's settling, seeing where and what we are as good enough. There's joy, hope, and vitality in choosing to keep growing. Philippians 4:4–9 offers strong support.

Choosing a growth orientation:

- *Helps our humility quotient.* It reminds us that we don't know everything, that we have much yet to learn (Rom 12:3; 1 Cor 10:12; 1 Pet 5:5–7).

- *Allows us to find at least some good in almost every situation.* Even if the overall situation is painful and sad, we will look for the parts that aren't. We'll ask ourselves the hope-filled questions. "What can I learn from this?" "How can this make me stronger?" (Rom 5:1–5). "How can I use this to help others?" (Phil 2:3–4). And "How is God blessing me even in these hard days?"

- *Invites us to treat others with respect and appreciation.* When we approach every encounter expecting to learn, we view the people we encounter as our teachers. We know to be careful; many people teach us what NOT to do. But sometimes we learn the most important lessons from the most unlikely teachers (Matt 22:34–40). Here's an example. In a local Captain D's a customer was rude to the staff. She got loud enough that the manager came out and tried to appease her. She was having none of that. All she wanted to do was to be heard by everyone in the place. The manager kept his cool and remained exceedingly professional. On our way out, I thanked him, saying, "It's a pleasure to see a professional at work. You handled that well." His attitude and approach both enhanced our dining experience and challenged me to follow his example.

- *Follows the teaching of 2 Peter 1:5–11.* We want every virtue to abound in our hearts and lives to the glory of God.

- *Makes it easier to deal with mishaps and delays.* We get to relabel them as adventures and unexpected opportunities to learn. It's amazing to see what God can do with and through situations that the world views as disasters. Think of Joseph's life, Moses having to leave Egypt, and Paul's shipwreck. Think of the cross. God is super at turning both lives and situations right-side-up.

- *Gives us strong reason to embrace life on earth for as long as God allows.* We're never through learning. We can show others how to keep learning. By continuing to "grow in the grace and knowledge of our Lord," we encourage others to do likewise (2 Pet 3:18). God is honored when we choose a growth orientation toward life and let His word guide our growth.

Staying Encouraged

Now David was greatly distressed, for the people spoke of stoning him, because the soul of all the people was grieved, every man for his sons and his daughters. But David strengthened himself in the Lord his God.

1 Samuel 30:6

Becoming discouraged from time to time is part of being human. Acting to prevent and overcome discouragement is part of being Christian. We who are "the salt of the earth" and "the light of the world" must "not be weary in doing well" (Matt 5:13–16; Gal 6:9). How can we prevent and overcome discouragement? Each of the following helps, but together, they invite God to work wonders:

- *Talk to God every day.* Pray humbly and honestly, "casting all your cares on Him, for He cares for you" (1 Pet 5:7).

- *Listen to God every day.* In addition to your regular program of Bible study, include a steady diet of especially encouraging texts (Psa 1, 23, 103, and 136; John 14 and 17; 1 Cor 15; Rev 21–22).

- *Sing praises to God every day.* Singing both incites and enhances joy (Jam 5:13; Acts 16:25).

- *Do something to encourage someone every day.* Help, affirm, notice, compliment, express appreciation, pray for, and speak to people. Acts 20:35 applies here!

- *Find joy in the good done to and by others every day.* Make their joy your joy (Rom 12:15; 2 John 4; 3 John 4). Joy shared is joy multiplied.

- *Count your blessings every day.* Most of us would struggle to count them all, but it's worth a try (2 Pet 1:3; 1 Thess 5:18). And don't forget to count the bad things that could have happened but didn't.

- *Soak in the beauty of God's creation every day.* "The heavens declare the glory of God, and the firmament shows His handiwork" (Psa 19:1). "He has made everything beautiful in its time" (Eccles 3:11). Think of sunrise, sunset, the shapes of the clouds, sky blue, green trees in winter, flowing streams, works of art, sweet words, the laughter of children, and the faces and voices and memories of those we love.

- *Anticipate the joys of heaven every day.* No death. No tears. No sorrow, No pain. No night. No separation. No needs. No struggles. No temptations. And God Himself will be with us forever (Rev 21–22).

God Knows Best

Command those who are rich in this present age not to be haughty, nor to trust in uncertain riches but in the living God, who gives us richly all things to enjoy.

1 Timothy 6:17

As we plundered in Birmingham for bargain books, we encountered many odd items. There were buttons, carvings, dolls, hats, posters, toys, and more. One of the biggest challenges of the day was to realize that all those things could live happily where they were; none of them had to come home with us.

None of them had to come home with us, but you guessed it. A few did. A thrift store had a tiny metal rocking horse and a pair of seashell bookends. Neither had a price tag, but I've learned that it seldom hurts to ask. The cashier asked her manager. His reply was, "One-fifty-nine." We were happy to buy them at $1.59 each.

Things, in and of themselves, don't bring joy. We know the famous saying of Jesus: "One's life does not consist in the abundance of things that he possesses" (Luke 12:15). We realize the danger of being owned by our things like the rich young ruler of Mark 10:22. Most of us realize the tragedy of valuing things above people and above God.

Kept in perspective, things can be both a blessing and an amusement. I hope you have experienced the joy of finding the perfect gift for someone you love. It combines adventure and providence with joy and giving. It makes for one fine set of memories.

My $1.59 things were not diminished by the fact that they cost so little. Quite the opposite. Part of their value was that they were so underpriced. I thanked the manager and meant it. There's quite a distinction between price and value.

As we left the thrift store, we needed go get back to the interstate for our trip home. I asked the helpful manager for directions, and he recommended backtracking a bit. Not being one to backtrack, I then quietly asked the cashier who checked us out. "You don't want to do that. Just take a right, stay in the left lane, turn left at the Shell station, and you'll be where you want to be." Turns out she was right on target.

I don't think for a moment that the manager was trying to mislead us. His route would have worked, but it wasn't the most direct and efficient. Yet, he was sure of it. Another old lesson has been re-taught so well. We can be sure of things that just aren't so. Think of Proverbs 16:25 and 21:2. I sure need help in weighing and testing my thoughts and actions. Or maybe the application is to think of Proverbs 15:22, "Without counsel, plans go awry, but in the multitude of counselors they are established." When the counselors are human, there's a place for listening more broadly and carefully weighing the words.

Speaking of being sure of things that just aren't so, this happened in a parking lot in Florence. I had just put the car in reverse and had my foot on the brake. I could feel us moving backward at a most uncomfortable pace. I mashed the brake even harder, and the feeling did not change. Turns out that a car was pulling into the space next to us, and my perception that we were zooming backward was completely wrong. It was yet another opportunity to recognize my limitations. Sometimes I don't know stop from go. Makes me even happier that God always knows and that He does so much to protect us, even from ourselves.

God With Us

In God I have put my trust; I will not be afraid. What can man do to me?

Psalm 56:11

66 "T"he Lord is my light and my salvation; whom shall I fear? The Lord is the strength of my life; of whom shall I be afraid?" (Psa 27:1) Why is that question so easy in the abstract? Why is it still a challenge when the hard times come? Why are we still surprised when the hard times come? Why doesn't the promise of life forever in the house of God permanently quell every fear (Psa 27:4)?

"Why are you cast down, O my soul? And why are you disquieted within me?" (Psa 43:5). Why do doubts still visit God's chosen? Why do we still have dark days that can turn into dark weeks, months, and years? Are those the wise questions to pose? What do we learn from a psalmist courageous enough to ask what he asked? What of the answers the psalmist offers? Do we know the dangers of reading half a verse?

"You, Yourself, are to be feared; and who may stand in Your presence when once You are angry?" (Psa 76:7) Do we still respect the terror of the Lord (2 Cor 5:11)? Do we realize that God cannot and will not abide evil—even our evil? Do we remember our upcoming appearance "before the judgment seat of Christ, that each one may receive the things done in the body, according to what he has done, whether good or bad" (2 Cor 5:10)?

In another vein, have we contemplated Psalm 76:7 in terms of the Lord's restraint? Do we consider both "the goodness and severity of God" (Rom 11:22)? With a thought or a breath from the Almighty, we could all be gone. Because of sin, we deserve that and worse. But the world stands and all the faithful "continue in his goodness" (Psa 33:8–9; Rom 11:22).

"Why should the Gentiles say, 'So where is their God?'" (Psa 115:2) Why do we consider it odd that many reject the God of the Bible? Aggressive unbelief is neither novel nor new. Why do humans continue to worship the work of their own hands? Shouldn't it be obvious why many prefer gods who can't speak, see, hear, or move?

"If You, Lord, should mark iniquities, O Lord, who could stand?" (Psa 130:3) Do we have the capacity to grasp the depth of our ruin without God's mercy? Do we have the wisdom to consider our fate without Him so as to better appreciate His love? Do we think of ourselves as "not so bad compared to others"? Do we see the folly in any hint of self-righteousness?

"Where can I go from Your Spirit? Or where can I flee from Your presence?" (Psa 139:7). Why do so many read just that question and miss the point? The psalmist doesn't want to flee. He knows there's no future in a life without God. On a logical level, we all know that it's folly to run from the omnipresent God. The point of Psalm 139:7 is stunningly positive. Could there be greater comfort than knowing God is always with us? Do we realize that He is ever near, doing more to help us than we dare dream?

SCRIPTURE INDEX

ABOUT THE AUTHOR

Bill Bagents is Vice President of Academic Affairs at Heritage Christian University in Florence, Alabama, and he serves as an elder and associate minister with the Mars Hill Church of Christ. He provides individual and family counseling as time allows and enjoys international mission work, teaching Bible and ministry, and writing. His wife, Laura, teaches sixth grade language arts. Their son, John, works in financial management in California. Bill and Laura lost their younger son, Allen, to illness in 2010.

CPSIA information can be obtained
at www.ICGtesting.com
Printed in the USA
JSHW051732270621
16132JS00003B/5